Contents

CW00393779

Published by
The Bible Reading Fellowship
15 The Chambers
Abingdon, OX14 3FE
United Kingdom
Tel: +44 (0)1865 319700
Email: enquiries@brf.org.uk
Website: www.brf.org.uk
BRF is a Registered Charity

ISBN 978 0 85746 098 1
First published 2014
10 9 8 7 6 5 4 3 2 1 0

Acknowledgments
Scripture quotations taken from The Holy Bible, New International Version (Anglicised edition) copyright © 1973, 1978, 1984, 2011 by Biblica (formerly International Bible Society). Used by permission of Hodder & Stoughton Publishers, an Hachette UK company. All rights reserved. 'NIV' is a registered trade mark of Biblica (formerly International Bible Society). UK trademark number 1448790.

Scripture quotations taken from The Holy Bible, New International Version, copyright © 1973, 1978, 1984 by Biblica (formerly International Bible Society), are used by permission of Hodder & Stoughton Publishers, an Hachette UK company. All rights reserved. 'NIV' is a registered trademark of Biblica (formerly International Bible Society). UK trademark number 1448790.

Scripture quotations taken from The New Revised Standard Version of the Bible, Anglicised Edition, copyright © 1989, 1995 by the Division of Christian Education of the National Council of the Churches of Christ in the USA, and are used by permission. All rights reserved.

Scripture quotations from *The Message*. Copyright © by Eugene H. Peterson 1993, 1994, 1995. Used by permission of NavPress Publishing Group.

Scripture quotations taken from the New Jerusalem Bible, published and copyright © 1985 by Darton, Longman and Todd Ltd and les Editions du Cerf, and by Doubleday, a division of Bantam Doubleday Dell Publishing Group, Inc. Used by permission of Darton, Longman and Todd Ltd, and Doubleday, a division of Random House, Inc.

Scripture quotations taken from the Contemporary English Version of the Bible, published by HarperCollins Publishers, are copyright © 1991, 1992, 1995 American Bible Society.

Scripture quotations taken from *The Voice* Bible, copyright © 2012 Thomas Nelson, Inc. All rights reserved.

Extracts from the Authorised Version of the Bible (The King James Bible), the rights in which are vested in the Crown, are reproduced by permission of the Crown's patentee, Cambridge University Press.

Extract from *As a Child* by Phil Steer, published by lulu.com, 2012

A catalogue record for this book is available from the British Library

Printed by Gutenberg Press, Tarxien, Malta

The Editor writes...

Welcome to *Quiet Spaces*.

As we begin this issue, we enter the summer, which gives the opportunity to meet God in different ways outside, enjoying his creation with him. With summer for many also comes travel, and so travel features in this issue.

Over the summer I find myself revisiting favourite haunts, and each time I find something new: a new place to explore, a different view or hidden gems I've missed before. Often our spiritual journey can be like this—revisiting passages and themes we've been to before, bringing new insights and a deepening relationship with God. There is a spiritual practice of repeating prayer exercises, and while I wouldn't recommend it every time, sometimes I reach the end of a prayer session and feel that there is further to go; God still has gifts to give me from this material; I still have something to learn and receive. At those times, I find it beneficial to return to the exercise at a later date, not to repeat what I have already covered, but to pick up where I left off and go deeper, allowing God to reveal his love and his truths further. Much of the groundwork will already have been covered, enabling me to enter God's presence more easily, ready to explore new places. Maybe over the summer you might have time to try this and to see where God leads when you give him the space.

In any one issue of *Quiet Spaces* you will find some repetition of similar themes or exercises. In this issue there are a few prayer walks, each with a different focus and approach, but you may find that using a similar route each time allows you to build on the time spent with God previously, and your walk might become a regular practice and place of prayer. There is also a focus on water, with the Holy Spirit and journeys over the sea, giving two very different approaches to similar themes.

So, as you journey through this issue, allow God, that trusted, safe and often surprising companion, to journey with you, to lead you, and to point out the sights and delights along the way.

Sally Smith

3

Writers in this issue

Anne Noble grew up on Merseyside and studied geology at Oxford and Toronto. She is a Team Vicar in Nottingham and is married with two grown-up daughters. In her spare time she loves gardening.

Lisa Cherrett is BRF's Project Editor and Managing Editor for the Bible reading notes. She sings in a choir, writes haiku when the inspiration strikes, and takes an interest in new forms of church, alternative worship and the relationship between Christianity and contemporary culture.

Sally Smith enjoys creating spaces that enable encounter with God through leading Quiet Days and creating prayer corners and stations. She has led prayer groups in her local church, works as a spiritual director and writes and produces education materials.

Andrea Skevington lives in Suffolk with her family. She writes for both adults and children, winning the Christian Book of the Year award (Speaking Volumes) for her retelling, *The Lion Classic Bible* (Lion Hudson, 2011). She also enjoys story-telling for children and running creative writing seminars for adults.

Bridget Hewitt lives in Northumberland. She is a wife, mother of grown-up sons, and daughter of elderly parents, all of which form the background to her involvement in spiritual direction and group work, travelling the spiritual journey alongside teenagers and adults. She has a Masters degree in Christian spirituality.

Helen Jaeger is the author of five books: *Paths Through Grief, As Night Falls, As Day Dawns, A Treasury of Wisdom* (Lion Hudson) and *Simple* (Scripture Union, 2003). She writes regularly for a variety of publications, including *Woman Alive* and for charities. Helen is also an editor, workshop leader and mentor.

Sally Welch is an ordained minister who lives and works in the centre of Oxford, working with families and young children in church. She is a writer and lecturer on spirituality and is particularly interested in pilgrimage and labyrinth.

Janet Lunt trained in music, composes, creates artwork and leads Quiet Days. She has designed several multisensory prayer trails, which have been used in Bristol, including in the cathedral, and beyond. With a colleague, she recently created a series of children's reflective corners for publication.

Sue McColough worked for a number of years at the BBC. She was then prayer coordinator at Tearfund, writing prayer materials and liaising with supporters. A reader at her church, she enjoys creative writing as well as organising and leading retreats and Quiet Days.

Dwelling in the Psalms

Anne Noble

Dwelling in the Psalms

The psalms are the praises and pleas of the people of Israel and express the heights and the depths of human emotion. They record the voices of individuals and communities as they wrestle with God through the challenges of life and faith. In them we too can find help in good times and bad, and learn more of the God who journeys with us through both.

Some key words recur in the psalms, and one of these is the word 'dwell', which is also translated as 'rest', 'live' or 'abide'. The idea of a God who dwells with us and in whom we can find a dwelling place recurs throughout scripture. In the Old Testament, God is described dwelling with his people in tabernacle and temple, and the Gospels speak of Jesus' incarnation as Emmanuel, God who dwells with us (John 1:14; NIV). The book of Revelation promises that God's dwelling place will once again be with his people—the new heaven and new earth where pain, death and tears will be no more (Revelation 21:3). Our scriptures express a longing to dwell with God for ever (Psalm 23:6).

In the psalms, dwelling places are described as places of life, safety, refuge, beauty, wisdom, joy, wholeness and peace (4:8; 27:4; 84; 85:9; 143). They are places to inhabit, places in which we may inquire of God and seek to know his depths. Our true home is with God and we merely sojourn elsewhere (84:2–4). Dwelling with God allows us truly to live and to live truly in all time.

God's dwelling place is lovely and desirable, a place of blessing. God's goodness and presence can sustain those who dwell with him even in wilderness places (68:7–10). His dwelling place is both close at hand and extends to the ends of the earth (65:4, 8). The whole earth is God's dwelling place (24:1–2). God's dwelling place in tabernacle and temple shines with his glory, full of holiness and beauty (see, for example, 27:4; 65:4). It is a place of salvation and new life where even deserts bloom and blossom (107). To dwell with God encourages a life of righteousness; those who practise deceit and evil cannot find a place to dwell in God's house (5:4; 101:7).

Meditation

Choose one of the verses or psalms referenced above. Read it slowly several times, both on its own and within the psalm as a whole. Note what unsettles or challenges you and try to lay this to one side (writing it down may help). Now notice what attracts you and what fills you with joy. Dwell with these things. Notice what God may be saying to you through these words.

Offer to God what you wish to say to him from this meditation.

The Father's house

Begin by reading Psalm 23. Through the words of John's Gospel, Jesus promises us that he goes to prepare a place for us in his Father's house (John 14:3), and he also assures us that he will guide us to that place. As you come to the final two verses of the psalm, imagine walking into God's dwelling place with Jesus beside you. Try to imagine the scene with all your senses. What or whom do you see? If you were to reach out, would your hands touch anything? What are the smells and tastes of the food on the table? What do you hear Jesus saying to you?

What would you like to say to him? How does it feel to be the honoured guest in God's house?

You might like to record your experience in words or pictures. Your thoughts don't have to be in fully formed sentences or finished works of art—single words and phrases or blocks of colour are just as helpful.

Prayer

Good shepherd, occasionally I catch glimpses of heaven on earth. Thank you for those moments when I experience your presence in everyday life. As I walk through the ups and downs of my life, may I know your presence beside me, guiding me always to that place where I may dwell with you for ever.

Reflecting on Psalm 23

The summer before last we visited Orkney. Both our children were about to leave home, and there was a sense of sadness as we realised that the nature of our family was changing. While we were there, we visited Barnhouse village in the Neolithic heart of Orkney, where people have lived for over 5000 years. It was a stormy day and the sky around us was a heavy grey, with funnel clouds forming on the cloud bases. Storms began to encircle us, yet at Barnhouse the air was perfectly still, so still that the lakes were mirror smooth.

Sitting in the ancient dwellings looking across the lake, I was reminded of the words of Psalm 23, which speak of still waters and green pastures as well as shadowed paths through hard places. All around, the turbulence of the clouds reflected the changes coming to our family. Yet in that moment and place there was a profound peace. I sat in houses thousands of years old contemplating an eternal God who had dwelt with his people for all time. I felt surrounded by God's love. Then, just as I experienced the peace of God's presence, I felt the faintest of breezes on the back of my neck and the first drops of rain. The eye of the storm had moved; rain was coming, yet the peaceful presence of God remained. To dwell with God forever is a promise for now as well as for eternity.

Spend some time in God's stillness, dwelling in his house and resting in his eternity.

Praying with Psalm 23

Read Psalm 23 slowly.

He leads me beside quiet waters (v. 2).

Take a bowl filled with water. Allow the surface of the water to become still. Thank God for the still spaces in your life. Now agitate the water. As you do so, watch how any reflections become distorted. It may be that as you stir the water you stir feelings of stress or storm within yourself. It can help to speak these out loud. Now let the water quieten again. As the surface quietens, imagine God's calming presence beside you.

You prepare a table before me in the presence of my enemies (v. 5).

Create a table laid out to welcome an honoured guest. Place on it your best or favourite plates, cups and cutlery. Perhaps you could add flowers or design a place card with your name on it. Then lay a place for God. Take time to do this as you welcome God as your honoured guest.

How does it feel to lay a space for God at your table?

What would you like to say to God as you sit together?

Now imagine the table God lays for you and the space he creates for you. How does it feel to be God's guest of honour?

If you feel able, invite your enemies to the table. How does it feel to sit with them? What might you say to them in this space?

If you can, leave your 'table' up for a while as a visual reminder that God dwells with you.

You anoint my head with oil; my cup overflows (v. 5).

Pour some oil on to your hands. Feel how rich and smooth it is. You might like to make the sign of the cross on your forehead or on the palm of your hand. Remember that you belong to Christ, that he dwells with you and you with him.

The word 'dwell'

In the middle of a sheet of paper, write the word 'dwell'. Focus on the word for a moment and write down around it any other words that come to mind. Stay with any words that have particularly struck you or that speak to you at this moment.

The *Oxford English Dictionary* defines the word 'dwell' in a number of ways. The verb 'to dwell' means to spend time, to abide or live in a place. I like the idea of inhabiting a space so completely that we know both it and those who share the space with us in detail.

To dwell can also mean to fix our attention on something or to write or speak at length—we dwell on ideas and thoughts, whether good or bad. Dwelling upon something that is bad for us can be harmful. On the other hand, dwelling on a word or phrase from a Bible passage allows us to attend to God and spend time with him.

Applied to horses, 'to dwell' means to pause before taking a fence or to be slow in raising their feet. There is something here about taking time and care before jumping or walking forward—the sense is to consider the next step or leap. If you are about to make a decision or choice, why not dwell in this way before you do so?

The noun 'dwell' is a slight regular pause in the motion of a machine. What a lovely idea! Do we have dwells in our lives? Whether or not we consciously fill such dwells with the practice of the presence of God, to pause regularly can be good for us.

Go back to the word association exercise that started this section. What do you notice about the words you wrote down? Are there others you might like to add? What might any of them say to you about the richness of dwelling? What do they say about your dwelling with God?

Building a dwell in our lives

In the previous section we saw that a 'dwell' is a 'slight regular pause in the motion of a machine'. As human beings we are far from simply being machines, but sometimes our lives can feel as though they have become mechanical. Perhaps we could develop a dwell so that we can intentionally pause in the routine to be aware of God's presence.

At home: set up a small space in a room you enter regularly—the kitchen might work well. Place in it something that will remind you to pause. It might be a favourite picture or a page from a book, or perhaps a verse from the Bible or other devotional text. You could put a note on a window that reminds you to stop and look out. It could be a piece of paper, some crayons, glue or collage material that encourage you to build a picture through time. Try to choose something that will attract your attention and appeal to you. The pause does not need to be for any great length of time; a few seconds in which you remind yourself of God's presence is sufficient.

At work: building a dwell into our working lives may be harder. Perhaps just turning your thoughts to God at the beginning and end of every working day might help. One suggestion is to use the door of your workplace as a trigger to prayer. Touch the door frame and know that as you enter the building, God is within. Ask for God's presence to dwell with you and bless your day and the colleagues you may have. As you leave, touch the door again and remind yourself of the words of Psalm 4:8 that as we go to rest, God will make us dwell in safety.

Dwelling in beauty

Read Psalm 27 slowly.

The psalm speaks of the psalmist's desire to 'dwell in the house of the Lord all the days of my life' and 'to gaze on the beauty of the Lord… to seek him in his temple' (v. 4). When we dwell in God's presence, there is both a place for simply gazing and for learning from him; inquiry (in the sense of the word 'seek') and contemplation result from a desire to find the dwelling places of God and linger there.

God's house guests bring adoring hearts and questioning minds, and, like Mary, we are allowed to sit at his feet and both learn from him and simply gaze. As a geologist I have beheld the beauty of the Lord while contemplating rocks, and I have found God in the knowledge that the meteorite in my collection was formed from material generated as our sun began to shine. Study and understanding may lead us to places of awe and wonder and to the place of contemplation. Taking time to understand something of the world around us gives us glimpses of the God who lies within. The whole of the earth and the wider universe are the house of the Lord. How much more, then, might we find God to be present in one another—the place where God's own image and likeness are to be found. If we take time to dwell both in places and with people, then we may discover God's presence both through contemplation and through understanding.

Prayer

Creator God, thank you for gifts of contemplation and inquiry. Help me this day to make time to seek you in your dwelling places within the world and in the people I meet, so that I may behold your beauty and learn more of you.

Praying through Psalm 27

The most repeated biblical commandment is, 'Do not be afraid.' Sometimes it is easier said than done to settle our fears. The writer of Psalm 27 has confidence that God's presence and light can keep fear out and boldly asks one thing of God, to remain in his presence by dwelling in the house of the Lord. For the psalmist there is sanctuary to be found in the temple—the place where God was believed to dwell amidst his people.

Here is a simple liturgy based on the words of Psalm 27.

Find a quiet place and read the psalm through slowly. Then say the words. If it helps, you might wish to hold before God one or two specific fears that you have.

Do not be afraid, I am your light.
   Lord, show me light in your face.

Do not be afraid, for I am your salvation.
   Lord, save me when I call upon you.

Do not be afraid, for I am your refuge.
  Lord, lead me to places where I may dwell with you.

Do not be afraid, for I am your dwelling place.
  Lord, help me to spend time in safety with you.

Do not be afraid, for you are beautiful in my sight.
  Lord, show me my worth reflected in your face.

Do not be afraid, for I will keep you close.
  Lord, sometimes you feel distant; Father/Mother, keep me close.

Do not be afraid, even when it looks as though there is none of my goodness in this world.
  Lord, lift my eyes, so that I may see where you are at work.

Do not be afraid; I will always be there when you call.
  Lord, give me courage to wait for you; may I dwell in you and you in me.

Lord God, help me to believe this day that you are my light and my salvation, my refuge and dwelling place. Amen

Psalm 4

Psalm 4 is one of the psalms set for the daily service of Compline, traditionally the final service of the day. For many, its words help the reader lay down the busyness of life in preparation to sleep safely, to dwell, in the protection of God.

The psalmist calls to God from a place where he feels hemmed in. It is a hard place and there are hints in verses 2, 4 and 6 that there is a struggle to find peace and prosperity of spirit in a busy, secular world in which other gods are trusted.

As you read Psalm 4, allow God to show you where you have felt troubled or boxed in by internal and external noise or pressure today. With the psalmist, cry out about these to God. If it helps, you might like to shout these out loud. Place any particular stresses and strains into God's hands. Imagine God holding them for you.

Now return to quiet and read the psalm again. This time, concentrate on the assurance of verse 8: 'In peace I will lie down and sleep, for you alone, Lord, make me dwell in safety.' Know that you are surrounded by God's love. You might like to lie down at this point and imagine God's protective arms around you. Receive his assurance. If you find this peaceful, stay with that feeling for as long as you are able. If you find later that you fell asleep, don't worry; take that as God's gift to you—a gift of peace for tired minds, bodies and spirits.

Prayer

Sometimes stresses and strains in life close in around me. I can so easily become imprisoned by them that I forget that their power to hold me has been broken by God in Jesus Christ. Lord, when I find that happening to me, help me to dwell with you and find that inner peace and joy which tells me that I am free in you.

Meditation on Psalm 4

In peace I will lie down and sleep, for you alone, Lord, make me dwell in safety.

PSALM 4:8, NIV

In this psalm, the word translated as 'peace' is the Hebrew *shalom*. *Shalom* is far more than peace; it is a sense of completeness that comes from dwelling with God, ourselves and our neighbours as part of a whole community. It carries a sense of harmony with God and the world.

Meditation

Imagine dwelling with God in *shalom*. Begin by relaxing intentionally. Slow your breathing. Starting with your toes and working through your body, tense each set of muscles in turn and then relax them. As you tighten them, hold before God the 'tight' places in your life, and as you relax them, let God open those spaces out in your mind. You may like to imagine God filling those spaces and making them his dwelling place.

Know that the Lord hears you when you call to him.

Imagine opening up a space of *shalom*—what would it have in it? What would make it a place of peace for you? Imagine the place filling with the presence of God. It is a place of wholeness, completeness and welcome.

Imagine yourself being welcomed into that space of *shalom*.

Lay before God those things that are on your heart, especially any that make you angry or cause you to tense up. As you let them go, imagine the *shalom* space opening up still more.

Rest for a while in this safe space with God.

Prayer

God of wholeness, you open up a dwelling space for me amidst the pressures and confines of this world. You open a door into a place of *shalom* where I may dwell in peace with you. Give me courage to hold open the door so that others may find freedom in its spaces too. Amen

You may like to write about or draw your place of *shalom* in your journal if you use one.

A liturgy of dwelling

God's dwelling place is holy, a place where justice and right-eousness, healing and wholeness are to be found. This liturgy reminds us of the promises God makes to us through scripture about his dwelling places. You might like to say all the lines out loud, or you could take one phrase and simply meditate on that. For those of you who enjoy writing, why not add more praises to God based on your own reflections.

Praise God who dwells among us in our sanctuaries, the holy spaces in our lives
Praise God whose dwelling place is filled with his glory
Praise God who dwells in the messy places of this world
Praise God whose dwelling place is filled with his love
Praise God who welcomes friend and stranger to dwell with him
Praise God who dwells with those who walk in his ways
Praise God whose dwelling is a place of holiness
Praise God whose justice dwells in desert places
Praise God whose dwelling is the place of righteousness
Praise God when his people flourish in the dwellings of his shade
Praise God whose dwelling is a place of peace
Praise God whose dwelling is a place of healing
Praise God who prepares a dwelling place for us
Praise to you, Lord God, for your rich dwelling place in our hearts
May we grow and flourish as we dwell with you.

Dwelling in the world with God

At the seaside, I love to search rock pools for the creatures that live there. It is a precarious existence, dependent on the tide's return. My favourites are hermit crabs. How wonderful that they find their homes in what is no longer needed by another creature! The shell protects the soft-bodied hermit crab. When it feels threatened, it can retreat inside, and wherever the crab goes it takes its dwelling place with it.

There is comfort in the knowledge that the places in which God abides are places of holiness, peace and beauty. Yet the psalmists also experience them as places of challenge. It is difficult to dwell in God's presence without being confronted by his justice and righteousness; qualities that urge us to face injustices and dishonesty in the world with his truth and love. How can we carry the love of God into the world and at the same time carry the sense of his protection?

Reflection

Find a picture of a hermit crab (the internet or local library might help) or go outside and find a snail, or use a shell you picked up when you were last at a beach.

Place the shell or picture where you can see it. Know yourself to be surrounded by the love of God, which is tender enough to envelop you yet tough enough to protect you. Imagine yourself curled up and completely held in that love as the creature is in the shell.

Now bring to God, in that safe, surrounded place, the concerns of your heart for those in the world. That might be people and situations close to you, perhaps even in your own life, or it could be much further from home. Where are these situations in the heart of God? Listen with all your senses to what God might be asking of you. It could be some specific action or prayer. If you feel afraid, remember that you dwell within the shell of God's love that surrounds you.

Take the sea shell or picture with you as you go about your daily life. It will remind you that wherever you go, God is there too.

You might like to record your thoughts and feelings in your journal if you use one.

Images of the Holy Spirit: wind and water

Lisa Cherrett

Nicodemus

John 3:1–10

The Holy Spirit, the mysterious third person of the Trinity, is hard to understand. Perhaps, in fact, we are not meant to 'understand' the Spirit with our rational minds. We cannot say what the Spirit *is*; instead, we must approach the mystery from different angles, asking, 'What is the Spirit *like*?' Ezekiel, in his vision of God, could only say that what he saw was, 'the appearance of the likeness of the glory of the Lord' (Ezekiel 1:28, NIV), and Jesus often talked about the kingdom of God in this way, saying, 'The kingdom of God is like…'. So what is the Holy Spirit like? Over the next fortnight, we'll be looking at two images that might take us deeper into an appreciation of the Spirit—wind and water.

Wind (or breath) and water are essential for life but, under some circumstances, both can be destructive, even life-threatening. Powerful forces that demand our full respect, they are constantly in motion, not easy to capture and hold still. If the Holy Spirit is like these unpredictable elements, we need to be prepared to be comforted and challenged in equal measure as we meditate on them.

We start with wind, and the story of Jesus and Nicodemus in John 3:1–10.

Nicodemus came to Jesus hoping to hear a word from God

(v. 2). He had already put his faith in Jesus to some extent, but what he heard that night was a complete puzzle to him. He was given no new law to follow, nothing concrete to do. Instead, he was asked to believe that the Spirit of God is like the wind that 'blows wherever it pleases. You hear its sound, but you cannot tell where it comes from or where it is going' (v. 8).

Sit quietly—outside if possible, especially if it happens to be a warm but breezy day—and read John 3:1–10. Imagine you are in Nicodemus' place and listen carefully to Jesus' words. What are your emotions? Bewilderment? Irritation? Fascination? Excitement?

Tell Jesus exactly how you feel and what you are thinking. He was eager to have a discussion with Nicodemus. Can you expect him to have a discussion with you?

'So loud a song'

I saw you toss the kites on high
And blow the birds about the sky;
And all around I heard you pass,
Like ladies' skirts across the grass.

Oh wind, a blowing all day long,
Oh wind, that sings so loud a song!

I saw the different things you did,
But always you yourself you hid.
I felt you push, I heard you call,
I could not see yourself at all.

Oh wind, a blowing all day long!

Oh wind, that sings so loud a song!

O you that are so strong and cold,
O blower, are you young or old?
Are you a beast of field and tree,
Or just a stronger child than me?

O wind, a blowing all day long,
O wind, that sings so loud a song!

'THE WIND' BY ROBERT LOUIS STEVENSON (1850–94)

This poem could be a response to Jesus' words about the wind. Stevenson describes how we feel it and see its effects in the sky and at ground level, even though the wind itself is invisible—just as the invisible Holy Spirit is active and powerful all around us.

Is the Holy Spirit singing a song to you? Try drawing a picture of the different things the unseen wind can do. Turn the poem, or your own picture, into a prayer of awe and wonder to God.

Bubble blowing

The wind, as it blows in the trees or between the buildings of a city street, is unpredictable and uncontrollable. Have you ever chased a piece of paper or a hat, as it was picked up and blown around by sudden gusts? It can be infuriating—but if you're able to stand still and simply allow the wind to 'blow wherever it pleases', you might find that you feel relaxed and liberated.

Sometimes we try too hard to predict and control and find solutions to difficult circumstances in our lives—or we come to the end of our tether and lose hope over a situation that seems to have become stuck in a rut, unable to budge, or closed off, dusty and airless. It might be a relationship that's gone stale, people who seem stubborn and unable to change, even for their own good, or perhaps a seemingly endless period of illness or unemployment. Sometimes we need 'a breath of fresh air' to blow away the cobwebs. It's at times like these that we really need the wind of the Holy Spirit to blow through.

Buy a pot of children's bubble mixture and take it outside. Relax and blow bubbles, watching them as they stream on the wind, float and finally burst. As you blow, name people and situations that need to feel the wind of God's Holy Spirit in a new way. Don't fall into the trap of trying to tell God how he must solve these problems or change the people involved. This wind is not under your control. You cannot trap it or hold it down or direct it. Simply hand over control to God and trust that it will blow in good and refreshing ways.

Jesus spoke to Nicodemus about the wind in answer to his question about how a person can be born again. As you pray, ask especially that the Holy Spirit would bring new birth to the people and situations you are naming.

A mighty rushing wind

The promised gift of the Holy Spirit, when it was given at Pentecost, did not come as a gentle breeze. As well as seeing flames of fire, the first disciples heard 'a sound like the blowing of a violent wind' (Acts 2:2). God's work can be comforting, but it may also seem threatening at times. The prophet Jeremiah was given a mission 'to uproot and tear down… to build and to plant' (Jeremiah 1:10). His calling from God was to both destruction and renewal.

The storm that hit southern England in October 1987 uprooted many trees, leaving sturdy trunks scattered across the roads as if they were spilt matchsticks. In the days that followed, though, experts suggested that the fallen trees were those whose roots were not as robust as they should have been. The storm winds went straight to those roots and sorted out the weak from the strong.

The Forestry Commission's website gives some insights into the long-term benefits of this kind of sort-out. When trees are uprooted in a storm, it creates 'gaps that allow the regeneration of trees and shrubs'; it produces 'open space and bright, sunny, warm conditions that allow flowers, butterflies and other insects to flourish'; it encourages 'the development of shrub habitats that will benefit birds and small mammals'; and it provides 'deadwood following the death of stumps, trunks and branches', which, again, makes good habitats for insects (www.forestry.gov. uk/thegreatstorm).

As Jeremiah knew, both uprooting and planting can be the work of God. Has the violent wind of the Holy Spirit been threatening to unsettle and uproot things in your life that seemed strong—material security, or old traditions and habits, mindsets and routines that look as if they should stand for ever, like ancient trees? In prayer, confess your fears about these unsettling events and think positively: what might God want to plant or regenerate in the spaces that are left when he has finished uprooting?

You might like to draw a sketch of a line of trees, with gaps, and write in some of the new life that God might want to bring in those empty spaces.

The breath of life

'Wind' and 'breath' are two different words in English, but there is just one word for both meanings in both Hebrew (*ruach*) and Greek (*pneuma*), the languages of the Bible. In Ezekiel 37:1–10,

God breathes into a pile of dead bodies and brings them to life, just as he breathed life into the first man, Adam, in Genesis 2:7. After thinking about the violent storm wind of Acts 2, we consider the gentlest manifestation of wind as an image of the Holy Spirit—gentle, but in its own way just as powerful as the violent wind.

Take some time to be still. Bring to mind something in your own or another person's experience that seems full of the gentle breath of the Holy Spirit—alive, upright, growing and maturing. Give thanks for the work of God that you see there. Think of something else that might seem dead, dry and hopeless. Hear God ask you the question he asked Ezekiel: 'Can these bones live?' What is your answer?

As you are settled in God's presence, spend a few minutes using a breath prayer. Choose one short phrase to pray as you breathe in, and another to pray as you breathe out. You might use the two phrases 'breathe on me' and 'breath of God', or choose your own.

Finish your prayer time by saying or singing this verse from the hymn by Edwin Hatch (1835–89):

> Breathe on me, breath of God;
> fill me with life anew;
> that I may love what thou dost love
> and do what thou wouldst do.

Harness the power

'The wind blows wherever it pleases,' but when its power is harnessed, its force is multiplied. Picture in your mind an old-fashioned ship on the sea, its sails filled with the wind, or a windmill or wind turbine turning with steady, rhythmic beat, or an eagle or glider plane riding the thermal air currents. Meditate on the ease and speed with which these objects move when they are driven by the wind, and the power that they can generate. You might like to watch a segment of a BBC programme with Sir David Attenborough observing the gliding flight of eagles (available on YouTube).

Alternatively, think of the way breath is harnessed by the voice or by a wind instrument to produce beautiful music. Perhaps listen to a piece of choral music or one that uses classical flute or jazz saxophone, or anything else of your choice.

In prayer, ask to become a person who is moved and energised by the power of the Holy Spirit. Can you find one object to remind you of this week's meditations? Place it where you can see or touch it through the day, and keep renewing your prayer for the wind of the Holy Spirit to empower you in whatever way you need most.

Drinking water

We move now into exploring water as an image of the Holy Spirit. In John 7:37–38, Jesus stands up at the end of the Feast of Tabernacles in Jerusalem (a harvest festival) and shouts out, 'Let anyone who is thirsty come to me and drink. Whoever believes in me… rivers of living water will flow from within them.' John goes on to explain that Jesus was talking about the Holy Spirit (v. 39, NIV).

Think for a few minutes about this picture of a flowing river. Like the air we breathe, water is essential for us: we cannot do without it. Also, like the wind, a river is always in motion. Stagnant water becomes unhealthy and deadening. Moving water is a delight to watch: it sparkles, reflecting light; it bubbles and froths, and makes swirling patterns as it flows over and around obstacles. Is this how you could imagine the Holy Spirit making himself known in your life?

Think now of Jesus' invitation to come and drink. I read these verses once at a time when I was at a very low ebb spiritually. (Notice the word 'ebb'—the exact opposite of 'flow'!) It struck me in that moment that drinking is one of the easiest acts imaginable. We do not have to understand God or the ways he works in our lives; we may feel as if the Christian life is just too hard at times, but Jesus invites us very simply to drink of him. The water of the Holy Spirit is a free gift (Isaiah 55:1).

Pour a glass of water—from a bottle or a tap, sparkling or still—and drink it. You may like to pray, 'Lord Jesus, I come to you and drink of your Spirit. May rivers of living water overflow from me today.' You could turn this into a rhythm of prayer through the day, to be repeated whenever you drink water.

The spring and the river

Jesus was standing on the steps of the temple when he spoke of the rivers of living water, which might have reminded his hearers of the prophet Ezekiel's vision of water flowing out from under the temple. Read Ezekiel 47:1–12 and drink in the vision of the gradually deepening water that becomes a life-giving, healing river.

A spring—the source of a river—is often tiny and hard to find, hidden in the rocks on a remote hillside. Yet it grows as it meanders downhill, eventually becoming a central feature of a town or city.

You may remember the film sequence shown on television at the beginning of the Opening Ceremony for the London Olympics in 2012: it followed the River Thames from its source in the Cotswold hills to the city of London. To be reminded, you could watch it again on YouTube.

In a few quiet moments, think of a project in which you or your church are involved. It might be intended to deepen the spiritual life of the congregation, such as a Bible study course, or it might be a way of connecting the church with its community—perhaps some form of social action, like Street Pastors, or an event for families, like Messy Church. Is the project just beginning, like a spring on a rocky hillside, or does it already have wide influence, like a river running through a city centre? Moving into prayer, thank God for this project and ask for his continued blessing on it. How might it increase its impact as a channel of the Holy Spirit in your church and local area?

Source or estuary—which captures your imagination and interest most fully? Are you called to be a pioneer or someone who joins the flow and helps it to increase? What does God want to say to you about this?

Confession

If you were to ask anyone to name the two main uses of water, they would probably say 'drinking' and 'washing'. The Israelites followed certain washing rituals before worshipping in the temple, and the water of baptism, for Christians, still carries the symbolism of cleansing from sin.

It could be helpful, as an aid to confession, to take a bucket of soapy water and a sponge or cloth outside and prepare to clean your car. As you look at the car, you'll probably notice that some parts are dirtier than others: it's quite likely that the windscreen is often wiped over, but the roof and doors become fairly dusty over time, and the bottom rim and wheel arches are grimiest of all. Allow God to bring to your mind the things you may have said or thought or done in the past day or two that need the cleansing of the Holy Spirit. Although all sin is serious, you might feel that some of the failings in your life are 'bigger' than others. Confess the small (perhaps a cross word to a family member, or a 'white' lie, told to smooth over a difficult situation) and the big (perhaps a general attitude of envy or pride). As you do so, sponge away the dust from the cleaner parts of the car, and then scrub the dirtiest areas. Finally, rinse the car with fresh water, and thank God for his forgiveness and cleansing.

Alternatively (if your car is already sparkling clean or if you don't have responsibility for a vehicle at all), you could use the daily washing-up routine as a similar exercise, confessing smaller shortcomings as you wash the cups and larger failures as you scrub the pans.

Rain from above

Read Job 38:25–27, which speaks of God as the one who causes the rain to fall.

Walking in a local park one lunch time, I noticed that the ground beneath the biggest tree had no grass. The bare patch extended as far on the earth as the branches stretched above, and I realised that I was looking at the area of the root system, which had sucked the ground dry and left no moisture to sustain the vulnerable grass on the surface. The tree relied on rainfall for its life, and there had been a long period of drought. Without rain, the tree itself could wither and die, like the grass in its shade.

Rain in the UK is often considered a nuisance: it spoils our summer barbecues, picnics and wedding celebrations. So we need to use our imaginations to understand how people in biblical lands would view rain—as a source of cooling refreshment in hot, dry conditions, and as a trigger for the germination and ripening of crops (the 'autumn and spring rains' mentioned in Deuteronomy 11:14).

The poem 'Thou art indeed just, Lord' by the poet-priest Gerard Manley Hopkins (1844–89) ends with the line 'Mine, O thou Lord of life, send my roots rain.' It's a prayer that I say for myself on the frequent occasions when I feel in need of refreshment and the power to be able to grow, flourish and produce some kind of 'harvest' in my life.

We all need the regular rain of the Holy Spirit to our roots. You could use the following pattern for your prayer:

When I feel stressed at the end of a busy day: mine, O thou Lord of life, send my roots rain.

When I feel bored by the routines of life: mine, O thou Lord of life, send my roots rain.

When people around me demand more than I can give: mine, O thou Lord of life, send my roots rain.

When I regret decisions of the past: mine, O thou Lord of life, send my roots rain.

When I fear decisions of the future: mine, O thou Lord of life, send my roots rain.

When I envy other people's joy: mine, O thou Lord of life, send my roots rain.

When old hurts rise up to haunt me: mine, O thou Lord of life, send my roots rain.

Water splashes

Spend some time simply watching the movement of water. Remember that stagnant water is unhealthy water: even the 'quiet waters' of Psalm 23:2 could not be stagnant or they would be undrinkable.

If you get the chance, sit by a river and watch it flow past stones and weeds. Stand by the sea and look at the waves: listen to the crash and sizzle they make as they break on the beach. Gaze at a fountain. Remember that we talk of a fountain 'playing': can you see what is meant by that? At home, you might play with water yourself, either alone or with a child. On the internet, you could search 'water droplets' on Google Images to see how photographers have captured the unique shapes that water makes in motion.

As you watch and meditate, do you gain a sense of the joy and energy of the Holy Spirit? How can you express that joy and energy to God?

Intercession

Praying for others can be frustrating when we see no results, even after many years—but when the Holy Spirit works, the landscape can be transformed in a moment. The following verses by H.W. Longfellow (1807–82) describe a dried-up river bed suddenly flooding with water because rain has been falling unseen elsewhere. The poem brings together the pictures of rainfall, springs (or 'fountains') and rivers that we have been thinking of in the past few days.

> As torrents in summer,
> Half dried in their channels,
> Suddenly rise, though the
> Sky is still cloudless,
> For rain has been falling
> Far off at their fountains;

So hearts that are fainting
Grow full to o'erflowing,
And they that behold it
Marvel, and know not
That God at their fountains
Far off has been raining!

Is there someone you've given up praying for, or someone you still pray for regularly and faithfully, but with less hope than in the past? Perhaps you could return to that prayer today, with the encouragement that each prayer could be another drop of rain that will bring a flood of God's Spirit, in his own good time.

As you did with the image of the wind, can you find an object that you could keep on display or within reach, to remind yourself of the Holy Spirit as water over the coming weeks?

Dear Lord and Father of mankind

Sally Smith

Introduction

In 2005 *Songs of Praise* held a poll for the nation's favourite hymn. 'Dear Lord and Father of Mankind' came second ('How Great Thou Art' came first). The words of this great hymn were originally written as part of a poem, *The Brewing of Soma* by John Greenleaf Whittier in 1872. Soma was a drink used in ancient Hinduism that is thought to have had hallucinogenic properties. Whittier was a Quaker, and in this poem he compares the frenzy created by drinking Soma to some of the Christian practices of the day in using 'music, incense, vigils drear, And trance, to bring the skies more near, Or lift men up to heaven!' In the final six verses of the poem, which later became the well-known hymn, he describes how Christians can find God without the need for Soma, by seeking stillness and listening for the still small voice of God.

Whittier's emphasis in the lyrics on silence, quietness and calm came from the practices of his Quaker faith. It is interesting that the poem is best known as a hymn, a form of which Whittier would have disapproved. So with this calm and stillness that Whittier intended, we enter the hymn over the next couple of weeks, using his words as a starting point for prayer and encounter with God.

The hymn begins by calling on the 'Lord and Father of mankind'. Who, for you, is this?

What would you offer as a counter to the frenzy of the modern world? What Christian practices would you suggest need countering? Hold these before God and ask to see them from his point of view. How does God see the practices of the church? How does he see your practices?

Reclothe us

Dear Lord and Father of mankind,
Forgive our foolish ways;
Reclothe us in our rightful mind...

The Bible uses the idea of a right mind in Mark 5:15 after a man had been cleaned of the evil spirits that held him. Being in a right mind can be linked to becoming the person God intended us to be. The demoniac in the passage, freed of the evil spirits, is able to become the person he was intended to be.

We may not be overtaken by evil spirits, but in the words of the hymn, we do have 'foolish ways'. What are your foolish ways? Think about those ways of behaving that, often with hindsight, you might consider to be less than perfect. Offer these to God, but also allow him to correct your view of your ways.

Then ask God for the counter to each of your foolish ways. It might be helpful to imagine God clothing you with the characteristics that will help you overcome the foolishness in you. Or you could draw a figure to represent yourself and add some clothes. What do the clothes represent? As you draw them, accept that gift from God. You could decorate the clothes with the words of the ways God would use to dress you. As you imagine or draw, allow God to clothe you and to make you the person he would have you be. Pause and acknowledge this new you, receiving it and giving thanks to God.

Thy service find

… In purer lives thy service find,
  In deeper reverence, praise.

St Ignatius devised a set of spiritual exercises for those wishing to join him in following Christ. In them he says, 'Man is created to praise, reverence, and serve God our Lord.' God creates us, loves us and wants to share our lives for ever. Our response to this love is to praise and serve God all our lives.

We are made by God. Everything around us is also made by God, and so our natural response is to revere those things and hold them precious as part of God's creation. In entering that love with God, our lives become purer, more centred on God and his desires for us. It is in entering into the life God has for us that we are freed to become the people he meant us to be, and to love and serve him as he intended. From the depth of the love come the praise and the service.

How do you serve God? Think not just of the things you do for the church, or the outreach activities you are involved in. How, each day, do you serve God?

In your mind, play back the last 24 hours and be particularly attentive to spotting how you have served God. You may recognise times when you have served his creation, in saving resources or helping others. You may see times when you have paused and praised God for his creation, or recognised something as having been made by God. Take each of these moments and offer them back to God, recognising his presence in your actions and thoughts. Recognise and thank God for his creation.

Over the next 24 hours, try to notice God's creation around you, his acts of love to you and to others. Recognise the opportunities presented to you to serve God in small ways and large.

Gracious calling

In simple trust like theirs who heard,
Beside the Syrian sea,
The gracious calling of the Lord,
Let us, like them, without a word,
Rise up and follow Thee.

Read Mark 1:16–20.

Imagine the scene; you are beside the Sea of Galilee. Feel the warmth of the sun. Enjoy the quietness. Look around at the water and the boats. What else can you see? What sounds do you hear?

You notice some fishermen in a boat close to the shore. Watch as they cast their net over the side of the boat, working together in well-practised ways. What might their lives be like? What does their boat tell you about their success as fishermen?

Then you see Jesus coming along the shore. He watches the fishermen for a while before shouting over to them, 'Follow me and I will make you fish for people.'

What do you think as he asks and they ponder their answer? How do they respond?

Then they bundle their nets into the boat, draw it up on to the shore and join Jesus, trusting in him.

While he waits for the fishermen, Jesus comes over to you and says your name. He invites you to follow him as well. How do you respond?

What else does he say to you?

What do you want to say to him?

How does it feel to be talking with him?

How willing are you to follow?

Spend some time with the Jesus who invokes trust in his followers and who has called you by name.

When you are ready to leave, you might like to replay the discussion you have had with Jesus. What surprises you in what you said and in what Jesus said?

Calm of hills above

> *O Sabbath rest by Galilee,*
> *O calm of hills above,*
> *Where Jesus knelt to share with Thee*
> *The silence of eternity,*
> *Interpreted by love!*

Several times in the Gospels we read of Jesus retreating to the mountains to spend time with God. In the calm of the hills above the lake he finds peace with his father (for example, Mark 6:46). Maybe he found it easier to connect with the creator when he was outside in creation.

Spend some time outside in creation and with the creator. Maybe sit in the garden or a local park in the evening, when human activity is stilling. Be still with the Father and share his enjoyment of what he has made; as we read in Genesis, 'And God saw that it was good.' Look and see that it is good. Listen to the noises around you. Beyond the noises, listen to the silence. Watch to see who else shares this creation. Look at the wonder of God's creation and see the beauty that would go unseen but for your eyes. Praise God for his world, for the richness and variety of the things he has put for us to enjoy. Receive the gifts God has for you in his created world.

Or, if you are feeling more active, go for a walk. Before you set off, ask God to show you his creation, and as you walk, be prepared to stop and look and praise when he does. Enjoy the richness of the variety and detail you see and hear.

You might like to respond to what you have seen and heard in silent adoration with the Father, or in creating a psalm of praise.

The silence of eternity

> … *The silence of eternity,*
> *Interpreted by love!*

We often think of eternity as stretching into the future. When I read of eternal life in passages such as John 4, I think of it stretching forward into eternity, and this idea of going on for ever becomes an easy concept, one I am maybe over-familiar with.

But what if we read Ephesians 1:3–6 and hear that God chose us before the creation of the world? Eternity stretches back in time as well as forward. Sometimes reading words in a different version can bring them to life in a new way. Ephesians 1:4 in THE MESSAGE version reads like this:

> *Long before he laid down earth's foundations, he had us in mind, had settled on us as the focus of his love, to be made whole and holy by his love.*

Or, slightly rephrased:

> *Long before he laid down earth's foundations, he had you in mind, had settled on you as the focus of his love, to be made whole and holy by his love.*

Reread this as you begin to recognise what it says and what that means about the relationship between you and God.

So, if we look backwards in time we see God's love for us was there before the world was even created. His love stretches back to infinity and forwards to infinity.

Read Ephesians 1:3–14. Try different versions to find one that speaks to you today. As you read it, again try changing the wording so that it becomes not a letter from Paul to many people but a letter from God the Father to you, personally and individually. It can help to add your name or to write it out in the format of a letter from God to you. Read it slowly, as such a love letter deserves, maybe keeping it in your wallet or purse. Allow the enormity of what God is saying to you to sink in. You may find that you only manage a few verses in one session and return to it again another day.

To end your prayer session, you might like to respond in a prayer letter or love letter to God. How do you reply to this letter he has sent you? What do you want to say to him, or is it beyond words, and you simply want to spend time being with God in the 'silence of eternity, interpreted by love'?

Let thy blessing fall

With that deep hush subduing all
Our words and works that drown
The tender whisper of thy call,
As noiseless let thy blessing fall
As fell thy manna down.

This verse is in the original poem, but is not always included in the hymn. It describes how easy it is to allow our words and works (however worthy) to drown out the tender whisper of God. How do we allow that deep hush that Whittier describes to subdue our words and work and so give God the silence and stillness to whisper to us and shower us with his blessings?

God provided manna for the Israelites in the desert and in the

Promised Land until they produced their own crops. Each day God fulfilled his promise to Moses; 'I am going to rain bread from heaven for you' (Exodus 16:4, NIV), and silently the manna fell each night for the people to collect.

How much more does God provide for us? And how much more does he want to give us good gifts?

Imagine arriving home one day and finding that the postman has left a parcel on the doorstep. It is addressed to you.

You take it in and remove the brown paper. Inside is a beautifully wrapped present. You read the label, which shows your name in beautiful lettering. It is from God. How do you feel?

Hold it as you anticipate its contents.

When you are ready, begin to unwrap it. Are you careful, or do you tear off the paper?

Inside is a box. You open the box and receive the gift God has for you inside.

How does this feel?

How do you respond?

You might like to pray your response, to write a letter to God. Thank him for his generous, gracious gift to you.

Sometimes we find the box is empty. Hold that emptiness before God, asking him what is in that emptiness and asking for eyes to see his grace and love. You might return to the box later, asking God what he has put in there for you. Or it might be appropriate to tell God what you had hoped would be in the parcel; lay before God that deepest desire of yours.

Strivings

Drop thy still dews of quietness,
Till all our strivings cease…

What a lovely image: God the Father carelessly letting drops of quietness fall until we stop striving and take notice of him. God is interested in and cares about our strivings. But he also cares enough about us to drop his quietness on to our strivings, not just once but repeatedly, until our strivings cease. Jesus told his disciples not to worry about what to eat or what to wear (Luke 12:22–34). God clothes the lilies of the fields and gives food to the ravens who do not store up food in barns. So, the God who loves us more than the birds or the flowers will not let us go hungry or be without clothes to wear. Instead, we should strive for the kingdom. He calls us to concentrate on serving him rather than ourselves. For those of us who naturally worry, this is a difficult passage; but imagine not having to strive, simply to allow God's dews of quietness to fall and to bring peace where there was striving. What we need to do is to become aware of these drops and to concentrate on them instead of on our worries.

Below are several images that can be helpful in seeing the dews of quietness. See which you can get hold of, and which brings with it God's peace.

You might find a gently dripping tap. Concentrate on the dripping and the rhythm of the water. Let the movement and the regularity take over as you watch and see the drops forming and falling, and landing. Become focused on the water until all your strivings cease.

Or take a handful of dry sand and allow it to fall from your fingers. Watch as it gently drops and builds up on falling. Feel the freedom of the grains and the space between them.

Or watch petals or dried leaves or seeds gently blowing in the wind. Watch them rise and fall and follow them on their aimless journey.

Whichever you choose, watch carefully. Feel the freedom and

the openness of the falling. Allow yourself to become totally involved in the action. Allow the action to take over from your strivings.

Then accept the peace God has given you as you join with the falling. Receive this gift from him.

The beauty of thy peace

> … *Take from our souls the strain and stress,*
> *And let our ordered lives confess*
> *The beauty of thy peace.*

We are often distracted from being able to receive God's peace by the noises within us; 'the strain and stress', as Whittier says. If we can get beyond those noises, we can make space for the beauty of God's peace; and with his peace he often brings order.

Pause and listen to the 'noises' inside you. These may be things you are in the middle of, jobs to remember to do, anxieties and worries, replaying events of the day (both good and bad), planning the next day…

Take each one and name it, recognise where it comes from, and then hand it to God, allowing him to look after it for you for a while, keeping it safe.

Whatever the noises are, offer them to God and allow him to bring some order to these aspects of your life. As each one is handed over to God, allow the space left to be filled with his peace, before the next noise enters and is dealt with in the same loving way.

When the noises stop, rest in his peace.

When you are ready, ask God to hand back the noises he wants you to take with you. Try to leave the others with God in his safe keeping.

Still small voice

Breathe through the heats of our desire
Thy coolness and thy balm;
Let sense be dumb, let flesh retire;
Speak through the earthquake, wind, and fire,
O still, small voice of calm.

Whittier returns to his main theme again in the last verse. We have distractions and desires that block our ability to hear the God who does not shout at us through the earthquake, wind and fire, but who whispers to us in a still small voice. We just need to be quiet enough, and to subdue the other noises, in order to be able to hear that still small voice. As a Quaker, Whittier was used to spending meetings in silence, listening for that still small voice.

Read 1 Kings 19 and imagine being with Elijah in the desert. Listen to him as he tells God about how alone he feels; how abandoned by God's people.

Watch as the wind comes and blows the sand. Listen to the noise it makes. Shield yourself from the sand. Hear also the emptiness of the wind without God.

Just as the wind is stilling, the earth begins to tremble and shake. Cling to the ground as it shakes. Watch Elijah look round for God in the earthquake, and again hear the emptiness.

See the fire break out and burn. Hear Elijah calling out for God. Listen and hear the emptiness. In the emptiness, share with Elijah in his loneliness.

And then all is still. No wind, no earthquake, no fire. Just stillness. With Elijah, you embrace the stillness after the commotions you have endured.

In the stillness you hear a tiny voice, calling your name. Respond to that call. Allow God to speak to you as you listen carefully to his still small voice. In the silence, tell him your greatest desire and receive his reply.

Still dews of quietness

Drop thy still dews of quietness…

For some people, silence is an old friend who welcomes them in. They long for it and readily know its value to them and feel bereft if they are not able to immerse themselves in it regularly. For others, silence is a place of fear, of the unknown. They fill it with noise and activity to keep at bay the demons that live in silence.

Opening ourselves to silence, though it can be challenging, can also be a revelation. If you are not used to silence, try this.

Find ten minutes and a quiet space where you won't be disturbed. Sit comfortably and rest. Become aware of the thoughts that are in your mind. For each one, acknowledge the thought and then lay it aside. Be aware of your body. Feel the muscles relaxing as the thoughts still. Gradually become aware of the noises around you. Don't respond to them, just be aware and then let them carry on. Notice your breathing, in and out, gently. Don't alter your breath; simply notice the rhythm of it. Then start to say 'Jesus' in time to your breathing. Concentrate on the word and feel it moving in and out with the rhythm of your breath. If your mind wanders, don't worry, that's normal; just put aside your thoughts and return to your breathing and the word 'Jesus'. With your in breath you can be inviting Jesus in; with your out breath, let go of tension and thoughts.

After ten minutes focus again on the things around you, on the noises of the room and the surroundings. Notice how you are feeling. Thank God for his still dews of quietness.

Try this as often as you can this week. Recognise how God is present to you and how you are able to hear his still small voice as the striving ceases.

Dear Lord and Father of mankind

Dear Lord and Father of mankind,
Forgive our foolish ways;
Reclothe us in our rightful mind,
In purer lives thy service find,
In deeper reverence, praise.

In simple trust like theirs who heard,
Beside the Syrian sea,
The gracious calling of the Lord,
Let us, like them, without a word,
Rise up and follow Thee.

O Sabbath rest by Galilee,
O calm of hills above,
Where Jesus knelt to share with Thee
The silence of eternity,
Interpreted by love!

With that deep hush subduing all
Our words and works that drown
The tender whisper of thy call,
As noiseless let thy blessing fall
As fell thy manna down.

Drop thy still dews of quietness,
Till all our strivings cease;

Take from our souls the strain and stress,
And let our ordered lives confess
The beauty of thy peace.

Breathe through the heats of our desire
Thy coolness and thy balm;
Let sense be dumb, let flesh retire;
Speak through the earthquake, wind, and fire,
O still, small voice of calm.

Reading the whole hymn, which lines stand out for you? Which lines have you found yourself singing over the past few days? You could take one of these and write it out to keep somewhere to remind you of what God has been saying. Or maybe you would prefer to find a way of depicting what for you is the essence of the whole hymn. This could be in words or art or dance.

If you have access to a recording of the hymn, you could use it (or sing the words yourself) to begin a time of silence.

The 'I am' sayings of Jesus

Andrea Skevington

Introduction

John's Gospel has a clear objective: that we who read it should believe 'that Jesus is the Christ, the Son of God, and that by believing [we] may have life in his name' (John 20:30–31, NIV 1984). John shows us no ordinary teacher, but one whose identity is revealed most powerfully in the 'I am' sayings that punctuate the text. We see that Jesus does not simply point the way, or speak truth; he embodies these things. Over the next two weeks we will explore the seven main sayings, and the life they bring us. Some scholars identify other 'I am' sayings, and if you have time to explore the whole Gospel, you may find them. Among them are John 4:26; 6:20; 18:5–8.

In each case, where Jesus says 'I am', he is echoing ancient words for God. The Old Testament has many titles for God, expressing different aspects of God's character. So too with these sayings: they reveal different aspects of Jesus' nature.

All the 'I am's of John's Gospel spring from the first I Am, in Exodus 3:1–17. Read it slowly, listening for what God is saying to you.

Is God calling you aside from your daily activities? Is God seeking to engage with you more deeply?

Think of the burning bush. How often do we feel burnt out, exhausted? This is not how it was with God's fire. Compare with Acts 2:3–4.

Read Exodus 3:4–15, noticing how God and Moses identify themselves. Is there an answer to Moses' question, 'Who am I?' (v. 11)?

What is God saying about his identity, his nature and his intentions?

What might it mean to find identity in God?

Remember Moses' story in Exodus; how his experience as a shepherd in this wilderness prepared him to lead his people; how bread, water, a way in the desert, life and light were all part of his story.

Reflect on times when you have felt far from God's path. Did anything good emerge from that time?

> *Earth's crammed with heaven,*
> *And every common bush afire with God;*
> *But only he who sees, takes off his shoes.*
> ELIZABETH BARRETT BROWNING (1806–61), *AURORA LEIGH*

'I am the bread of life'

John 6:1–59

Try the following meditation while making bread. If you don't have time for bread making, you could simply use the final section, 'Breaking and eating'.

Preparing and mixing: as you gather and mix your ingredients, hold in your mind Jesus' words: the mustard seed (Matthew 13:31–32, and 17:20), the growing seed (Mark 4:26–27), the parable of the sower (Luke 8:4–15), yeast (Luke 13:20–21), a seed falling to the ground (John 12:24). As you work, relate these to Jesus, who said, 'I am the bread of life' (John 6:35).

Kneading and rising: as you knead the dough and leave it to rise, continue to dwell on those words. Think how things have their own timescale; how grain takes time to reach fruitfulness. Consider how God chooses to involve us in his work, such as the kneading, but the growth is his. He requires patience.

Knocking back: what must it have been like to receive manna, God's provision in the desert (see Exodus 16:1–17)? Enough for each day, even in barren places.

Second rising: consider John 6, the feeding of the 5000. Dwell on God's abundant provision.

Baking: as the smell of bread fills your home, what does it mean for you to feed on Jesus daily? How is Jesus your bread of life?

Breaking and eating: perhaps you can share your bread. How can Jesus be the bread of life in your community? Are there practical ways in which you, and your church, can show love and care? In my own church, we open our building to the community for a toddler group. It is growing. There are enough volunteers to make sure that no one has to sit alone, and from conversation flows friendship and prayer. The toaster is always on, the church is full of the smell of toast, and we share bread together.

Pray a prayer of thankfulness over your bread, and ask God to sustain you and others through it, and through Jesus, the bread of life. End by reading Luke 24:30–32.

'I am the light of the world'

John 9:1–12

In dark times, words of truth can sustain us. It is good to have some in our memory. Read the prologue to John's Gospel (1:1–18), looking for one or two verses about light or glory that stand out for you. Write them down on cards and pin them about the house as you begin to learn them by heart. Then read the first few verses of Genesis. Note how John echoes the great divide between darkness and light, and try to add some more words to your memory: 'And God said, "Let there be light," and there was light...' (v. 3).

Then, find a place you can make dark and sit down, keeping a candle and matches within reach. Give yourself time to adjust to the darkness. Sink into it. What do you hear and smell and feel? What do you see? Are there sources of light you can't shut out—streetlamps, others in your household, neighbours or moonlight? What does it mean to receive traces of light from others? What experiences have you had of utter darkness? Pray for those who live in darkness.

In the darkness, try to recall the words you have learnt, breathing with them, dwelling on them. End by lighting a candle, and again recall the words, 'I am the light of the world.'

> **Darkness cannot drive out darkness; only light can do that. Hate cannot drive out hate; only love can do that.**
> MARTIN LUTHER KING, JR. (1929–68), *STRENGTH TO LOVE*

'I am the light of the world'

The Quaker tradition of meditation is very rich. I encountered this at an exhibition of needlework in the Lady Chapel of Ely

Cathedral, with each piece telling the story of Quakers who had blessed others through science, business, education and campaigns against slavery and violence. This small community has done good, sustained by a corporate discipline of waiting on God. The Society of Friends has many resources for those who wish to find out more. *Light to Live By* by Rex Ambler (Quaker Books, 2008) provides an excellent starting point. The founder of the Quakers, George Fox, devised a set of principles for prayer. This exercise is based on those principles and the theme of God as light. Work slowly through these points. Pause where you find God. It may take several sessions—or even a lifetime.

1. **Look inside.** 'Your teacher is within you. Mind that which is pure in you to guide you to God.' Mind the light.

2. **Identify the light.** 'Now this is the Light with which you are lighted, which shows you when you do wrong.' When you bring yourself into the light, you see your troubles, your temptations, your wrongdoing before you.

3. **Let the light show you yourself.** 'Mind the pure light of God in you,' which shows the things in you that are not light; let your conscience be stirred. Awake from sleep, let the light of Jesus Christ search you.

4. **Trace the light to its source.** Stand in God's counsel, learn from the light so that 'you may be led forth in his life and likeness'. Wait for God to restore his image in you.

5. **Trust the light to show you the alternative.** Have courage to stand still in the light; it is the light of your Saviour. This is the first step to peace; grace grows here. For looking down into sin you are swallowed up in it, but looking at the light that

reveals sin, you see above and beyond the light.

6. **Feel the new life grow.** 'He who follows the light comes to have the light of life.' The Lord has sown a seed in you that lies shut up in the darkness, with winter storms about it. He sends his light to the seed, that with time the new life will grow.

7. **See other people in the light.** Abiding in the light, you will see the unity that is amongst you, for in the light no self-will, no mastery can stand. We are all equal before the light.

8. **See the world in the light.** This light lets you see all the world as it is, and keeps you mindful of God.

9. **Learn to love in the light.** Standing in the eternal power and light of God, we have strength to love those who persecute and wrong us; we have light enough to shed light on the paths of those who are against us.

'I am the gate'

John 10:7–10

John 9 to John 10:21 contains interweaving threads of true sight and light, and good and bad spiritual leadership.

In these verses Jesus is talking to the Pharisees, whose pastoral care of the man born blind has been so poor. Jesus is the gate for the sheep, offering both safety and adventure. A Middle Eastern sheepfold was encircled with stone walls, and the shepherd lay across the entrance at night to keep his flock safe. We too can be at peace, a sheep of his flock. But a flock remaining in the fold will soon sicken, so the gate is also the way out for the sheep, who follow the shepherd to good pasture. That balance of resting in the fold and following Jesus out into the world is life-giving.

Consider Jesus' promise of abundant life, and give thanks for where you see abundance in your life. Ask for a greater measure of this abundant life.

At this season of your life, consider this balance between safety and adventure, enclosure and stepping out. Are there new gates opening for you?

The sheep listen for the shepherd's voice (John 10:3–5). Listen for the shepherd's voice and let him guide you.

Doorways and gateways

Doorways and gateways, both actual and metaphorical, are significant places (Deuteronomy 6:6–9; Exodus 12:22). Think about doorways you pass through daily. Can you mark them in some way, to help you remember Jesus, the gate? Can you develop the habit of praying when you pass through the doorway of your home, place of work, school, or shops?

Take photos of doorways and gateways, using the lens to help you see differently. What is beyond the gate for you? Use your photographs to prompt prayer.

Study artwork where glimpses are seen through doors and windows. Many Renaissance paintings and Dutch interiors show snatches of life beyond the central subject. Think about your own life. What can you glimpse? Draw or photograph half-hidden views through your own windows and doors.

Here is a poem I wrote after suddenly noticing an old door on a familiar route. Behind it was a wonderful place, where the poet, Bernard Barton, was buried. Perhaps there are doorways you could write about too.

Quaker burial ground: the door

This narrow lane, these close brick walls,
shut out all but a thin strip of sky,
forcing the eye, and the mind, onwards.
So, each day, we rush past the door
as if it were invisible, enchanted.

Perhaps it was the sudden startle
of a blackbird, or a gust of wind
rising over the wall, or a simple
opening of the eyes, but there it was:
peeling layers of paint,
a round handle snug in the palm,
the scrape of splintered wood on stone,
a sudden burst of light.

And we turned aside from our path,
stepped into a cool fire of shining green,
crucibled in crumbling walls.
In this place of prayer, of birdsong,
green daffodil heads bow,
while comfrey uncurls,
and thick grass sways
silver in the breeze.

And the soft rows of plain
grey gravestones lie buried
in the rising rush of green,
where all—the door,
the living growth,
the gentle words
carved on graves,
speak resurrection.

'I am the good shepherd'

John 10:11–21

As we read these verses, we see once more how Jesus is contrasting his role with that of the hired hand—those who seek spiritual leadership for reward.

Jesus' hearers will have called to mind the many Old Testament passages that dwell on the shepherd, and understood Jesus' meaning. Read through some or all of the following Old Testament examples of the Shepherd, and think what it means to you to trust in God, and to be guided. Where is the Good Shepherd leading you today? If you have any kind of leadership role, how can you better follow his example?

Here are some examples: Isaiah 40:11; Isaiah 63:11–12; Jeremiah 23:4; Ezekiel 34:1–16; Psalm 23; Psalm 28:6–9; Psalm 80:1–3.

Responding to the Good Shepherd

Use one of the following to respond to the call of the Good Shepherd, taking time to remember God's leading in the past and to ask him to guide you on the way ahead.

Music: listen to music on this theme, for example settings of 'The Lord is my Shepherd', 'All the Way my Saviour Leads Me' or Handel's *Messiah*. Sing, play or dance as you worship the Good Shepherd.

The road of your life: write, draw or paint the road of your life so far. See this exercise as a form of prayer, something you share with God, asking him about each stage of your journey. Are there times when the Good Shepherd guided you, although you were unaware of it? Remember Moses, the adopted prince who ran away and worked as a shepherd. It was there he learned to lead his people to freedom. His story teaches us that even seemingly lost years are not lost, and also teaches us to look back on those who have guided us, as Moses guided his people, with thankfulness.

You could use this two-voice presentation as your prayer response. Cry out to God and receive his promises.

I am the Good Shepherd. My sheep are scattered over the stony hillside, and I will seek them.

> *I look for you, I thirst for you, in this dry and weary land.*
> *I am alone in this desert place, like a sheep without a shepherd.*

They lost their way in days of cloud and darkness, and I will find them.
They fell into dangers, alone, and I will rescue them.

> *My heart grows faint, and hope flies away from me like a bird at evening.*
> *How I wish I had wings, and then I too could fly away.*

I will find the lost ones, the lonely ones, and I will gather them to my heart.
I will feed them like a shepherd, and carry the lambs in my arms.
I will gently lead those who have young.
I will bind up the hurt, and strengthen the weak.
I do not grow tired or weary,
And I love them with an everlasting love.

> *Do not keep far from me, O God. Have compassion on me.*

Do not be afraid, I call you by name, you are mine.
  Hear my cry, O God, listen to my prayer.

I am with you even when deep waters would sweep you away.
You are precious in my sight. I do not leave you alone, or forsaken.
I will come to you. I have come to you.

'I am the resurrection and the life'

John 11:1–44

As we read through this many-layered passage, we see life and glory emerge from the shadow of a cave-tomb. In her grief, Martha makes her confession of faith in Christ, and as Jesus weeps by the tomb, he calls on his Father. Then we, along with Martha, see the glory of God. This passage is the tipping point into the Easter narrative. In it, Jesus declares himself to be the life that is greater than death.

We narrow our focus to one half verse, and use it as a starting point for prayer. 'Jesus said to them, "Take off the grave clothes and let him go"' (v. 44b).

What do grave clothes mean to you?

Firstly, imagine yourself bound, hand and foot, as Lazarus was, with a cloth over your face. You might wish to use a strip of cloth and enact it. What does that feel like? What impact would it have?

Now, think of those things which may be 'grave clothes' in your life: fear, debt, disappointment or bad habits. Take your time, and ask Jesus to release you.

Next, ask Jesus if there are any known to you who are bound in this way, and pray for them. Expand your prayer to your community, and ask Jesus to set it free from its bindings. Ask if there are practical things you can do to set people free.

If you have used a strip of cloth, cut it, and keep it as a bookmark to remind you of your freedom.

'I am the resurrection and the life'

If you have time, read on from the raising of Lazarus (John 12—13; 18—21), seeing how that event influenced what followed, remembering the themes of life and light of John's Gospel.

In your own story, when can you see Jesus bringing resurrection, light and life? Has God been at work in your own times of shadow and darkness?

Wendell Berry's poem 'Manifesto: The Mad Farmer Liberation Front' (*The Gift of Gravity*, Golgonooza Press, 2002) ends with the line 'Practise resurrection'. Those words have been used by Shane Claiborne (*The Irresistible Revolution*, Zondervan, 2006; see also www.thesimpleway.org) and others to characterise their resolution to live out the resurrection life, including the renovation of derelict housing and urban wasteland farms as modern examples of making waste places rejoice (see Isaiah 51:3).

Ask God whether there are ways you could 'practise resurrection'. God delights in using the flawed, the old and the cast aside, like Moses or Abraham. Remember how 'he who was seated on the throne said, "I am making everything new!"' (Revelation 21:5, NIV 1984). Ask Jesus to bring his resurrection life into your life now, to breathe into the dead and dark places; similarly ask this for those you love, and for your community.

Where could you be part of this process of making all things new, bringing new life?

Start simply—renew an old, thrown-away object, restore a piece of furniture, reuse old fabric for a sewing project, plant vegetables in a neglected place, make compost, use broken plates for mosaic, make something beautiful out of what has been cast aside.

'Practise resurrection.'

'I am the way, the truth and the life'

John 14:6

The disciples were lost, confused, terrified. In these words, Jesus did not point to an answer; rather, he showed that he is the answer. Once again we see that out of losing comes finding, for unless Jesus goes ahead, their rooms will not be prepared, and the Comforter cannot come to them.

Pray for truth and life as you walk your everyday routes. Alternatively, you might use local maps and newspapers to pray for your area.

As you walk, be mindful of Jesus, the way, with you. Be thankful, and worship. Ask him what he sees, and listen for answers.

Jesus spoke these words at a distressing time, so pray as you walk for those in distress, that they may be comforted. Pray peace and blessing on homes you pass. Pray for truth and life. Pray too for businesses, for dark alleyways, for green places, for roads and railways. Pray truth and life for all the ways you pass down.

Try to develop a habit of using your travelling time to be open to God, to what is going on around you, and to pray.

'I am the true vine'

John 15:1–17

It seems that Jesus spoke these words as they walked through darkness to the garden of Gethsemane (14:31; chapter 17). Maybe they passed pruned vines beginning to shoot, and Jesus' words charged the everyday with meaning: the vine—fruitfulness, abundance, God's provision, the symbol of Israel (1 Kings 4:25; Psalm 80:14–15; Isaiah 5:7).

Read Ephesians 3:14–19 and Galatians 5:22–23, holding in mind what they have to say about community and fruitfulness.

Jesus, you are our true vine.

Keep us rooted in your love.

Jesus, you are the life that flows through us.

Keep us open to you.

Without you, we wither.

Help us to understand your pruning.

Without you, we cannot bear fruit.

Help us to recognise your cleansing.

We long to be fruitful for you.

You command us to love one another.

Give us strength and grace to love.

The branches of the vine entwine and support each other.

Help us know that we are one in you.

In you is abundance of life.

In you is the fruitfulness of the grain that falls to the ground.

Bring forth fruit in our own lives.

In you the grapes ripen in the autumn light,

And the fields are white with harvest.

Deepen your image in us,

So our lives bear the fruit of your spirit.

Love, Joy, Peace, Patience, Kindness, Goodness, Faithfulness, Gentleness, Self-Control.

Amen

Meister Eckhart

Bridget Hewitt

Who was Meister Eckhart?

Meister Eckhart lived from approximately 1260 to 1328 in Germany. He was a member of the Dominican order, and a great theologian, revelling in the exciting new strands of thought (Jewish and Muslim as well as Christian) that were emerging during those centuries. He travelled on foot across much of northern Europe, discussing, learning and teaching alongside both academics and also the considerable variety of religious women of his time. He wrote (in Latin, the language of learning) and gave sermons (in German, the language of ordinary people); and all the time he was communing with God, entering into the living, dynamic, vibrant *reality* of God. Eckhart met with God at every turn of life, and he used every device of word-play that his active mind could invent to try to communicate his experience. Sadly, towards the end of his life, some of his work was criticised and eventually condemned as heretical. In the last hundred or so years, however, his writings have come increasingly to light, and he has been recognised as a great mystic, speaking a deep and resonating language that can set souls on fire.

Eckhart often writes in riddles and poetry, which are not always easy to understand. In the days that follow you may find the best way to pray with him is simply to 'chew' on his words, a bit like chewing the cud. If his words don't work for you, don't worry: he doesn't necessarily speak to everyone. The important thing is to use what speaks to *you*, not to worry about what doesn't.

In prayer today, let's simply imagine. Imagine the wind

rippling through reeds on a warm spring day. Imagine a sunset over a calm sea, sending its rays of colour rippling towards you. Imagine the plaintive call of wild geese as they set off on their long journey to the north. Imagine anything that calls to you from the great beyond, anything that sets *your* soul on fire; any moments when you feel the call of eternity.

Become aware of this call, deep within you.

The eternal birth of God

The theme of the eternal birth of God is an Eckhart 'hallmark' which we shall dwell on over this fortnight.

All quotes by Meister Eckhart are from the following book unless otherwise stated: Walshe, M. O'C. (ed.), *Meister Eckhart, Sermons and Treatises, volume 1*, Element Books, 1987.

Eckhart takes the story of Jesus' birth as his starting point, but knows it as so much more than a historical event.

'Where is he who is born king of the Jews?' asks Eckhart (quoting from Matthew 2:2), and continues, 'This eternal birth occurs in the soul precisely as it does in eternity, no more and no less, for it is one birth... Just await this birth within you' (p. 15).

As we pray today, we want to allow space for Eckhart's words to resonate within us.

Sit quietly and breathe gently.

Breathing in, feel God entering your being; breathing out, feel yourself letting go of tension.

And so again and again, breathe in, letting God's fullness enter your being, and out, letting go of thoughts and tensions that arise.

Your thoughts will wander, but as you come back to God each time you breathe consciously in, you will be making space for God.

As your body quietens, let Eckhart's words flow through you:

'The eternal birth... happens daily in the innermost part of the soul' (p. 25).

God

God, for Eckhart, is eternally self-giving and cannot help but give birth. His very being depends on his birth-giving. 'The word "father" implies pure begetting... His being depends on His bringing His Son to birth in the soul, whether He would or no... He does nothing else but beget His Son' (p. 285).

God's fecundity, God's creativity, God's fertility, is of the very nature of God. God *is*, in order to eternally give birth, eternally bring forth something new. ('Look, I am doing something new,' Isaiah 43:19, NJB.)

There is something extraordinarily beautiful in this picture of God, something that calls us to respond.

What is God calling to be created in you? What is waiting to be born?

In prayer today, give time to drawing or painting, letting the image of the birthing God present itself to you in whatever way this comes.

Don't worry about results: simply play with colour, with words, with the whole idea of creating.

Let your heart respond to the freedom of paper and colour.

Ask God to show you what is being born within you.

The soul

For Eckhart, God and the soul are often two sides of the same coin. It is God's nature to give birth: it is the soul's nature to receive it. The birth happens in 'the ground... the very essence of the soul which is the soul's most secret part' (p. 3). Just as

God 'is never content till He begets His Son in us, [so] the soul too is in no way content until the Son of God is born in her' (volume 2, p. 157). Eckhart is perhaps alluding to a sense of 'longing' that sits within the human person, a longing that can ultimately be met only by God.

Today, go out into a garden or park, and just look. Look at the branches and twigs of a tree, leaves unfurling, flowers pushing through the soil. Spend some time looking. See the beauty. See at times the strangeness or even the ugliness. Let the wonder of growing things seep into your being. Let yourself be touched by wonder, by old things, new things, birth, death, the cycles of life, and know that there is a world greater than you can conceive of. When you are back inside, you might like to jot down any thoughts or words that have come to you.

You might like to ponder the following passage:

> I have sometimes said that there is a power in the soul which alone is free. Sometimes I have called it the guardian of the spirit, sometimes I have called it a light of the spirit, sometimes I have said that it is a little spark. But now I say that it is neither *this* not *that*; and yet it is a *something* that is more exalted over 'this' and 'that' than are the heavens over the earth. So now I shall name it in nobler fashion than I ever did before, and yet it disowns the nobler name and mode, for it transcends them. It is free of all names and void of all forms, entirely exempt and free, as God is exempt and free in Himself. It is as completely one and simple as God is one and simple, so that no man can in any way glimpse it. (volume 1, p. 76)

Eckhart is speaking about something he knows and longs to share. We cannot 'make sense' of this; it will speak clearly to some people, others will have to sit with it and allow it to enter deeply and work in them, yet others may prefer to stay with the wonder of growing things they experienced earlier.

Leaving the crowd

Eckhart has an intoxicating and almost light-hearted way of giving familiar Bible stories a different slant, opening our eyes and ears to them in a new way.

Read the story of Jesus in the temple at the age of twelve (Luke 2:41–50).

As we know, Jesus' parents could not find him among their friends and relations. Eckhart tells us:

> They had to go back to where they had come from…
> And so in truth, if you would find this noble birth, you
> must leave the crowd and return to the source and
> ground from whence you came. All the powers of the
> soul and all their works—these are the crowd. Memory,
> understanding and will, they all diversify you, and there-
> fore you must leave them all… After that, you *may* find
> this birth but not otherwise—believe me! He was never
> yet found among friends, nor among kindred or acquain-
> tances: there, rather, one loses him altogether. (p. 39)

Read the passage from Luke again in the light of Eckhart's retelling of it.

What are the 'friends', 'kindred', 'acquaintances' in your life that may be preventing you becoming aware of the birth of God in your soul?

Sometimes we have familiar ways of operating, familiar patterns of thought, that need to be broken open, shattered, in order for us to let God in.

Sometimes there are familiar things that pull us down, often covered in cloaks of acceptability.

Spend some time with this story, asking God to show you where and what are the over-familiar patterns in your life that you may need to put aside in order to return to the truth of who you really are, to meet God's presence within.

The eternal now

The birth of God happens in the soul eternally, always *now*. 'The eternal Father is ever begetting His Eternal son without pause' (p. 74). The timeless eternity in which the birth happens brings together Eckhart's teaching on both God and the soul, and shows how they are intertwined:

> All time must be gone when this birth so begins, for there is nothing that hinders this birth so much as time and creatures… If the soul could be touched by time, she would not be the soul, and if God could be touched by time, He would not be God… If it were possible for the soul to be touched by time, then God could never be born in her…
>
> The soul in which God is to be born must drop away from time and time from her, she must soar aloft and stand gazing into the richness of God's [creation]: there is breadth without breadth, expanseless expanse. (p. 216)

Eckhart is talking here about the importance of living in the present moment. In another place he writes of 'receiving the divine gift in the eternal Now' (p. 58).

How do we live in the present moment?

Do we really want to?

Most of us can only do this for short periods, but even to practise it for short times helps to put other aspects of life into perspective.

Look at the last sentence of the paragraph above: 'The soul in which God is to be born... must soar aloft...'

Imagine an eagle soaring over the landscape: let your soul too, soar aloft into the infinity that is God. Feel the extraordinary vastness of God's love

surrounding you,

holding you,

loving you just as you are.

Feel your everyday cares slipping from you.

Feel the littleness of daily anxieties.

Feel the enormity of love surrounding you, calling to you.

Feel the enormous space and freedom that is God.

Let Eckhart's poetic language take you where it will, and give thanks.

Jesus clears the temple

Matthew 21:12

In his sermons Eckhart has a habit of returning in different guises to his favourite themes. Again, this is a well-known Bible story, and Eckhart asks why Jesus was so keen to clear the temple: 'For this reason God wants this temple cleared, that He may be there all alone' (p. 55). He goes on to explore the fact that the people buying and selling in the temple were not necessarily bad people, but they had attachments; they wanted by their actions to gain God's esteem. So he goes on:

> If anyone else would speak in the temple (which is the
> soul) but Jesus, Jesus is silent, as if he were not at
> home... If Jesus is to speak in the soul, she must be all
> alone, and she has to be quiet herself to hear what he
> says. Well then, in he comes and starts speaking. What
> does the lord Jesus say? He says what he *is*. What is he
> then? He is a Word of the Father. In this same Word the
> Father speaks Himself, all the divine nature and all that
> God is. (p. 59)

There is so much packed into these words that we need to spend
a while with them.

First of all, simply reread Matthew 21:12, this time imagining
the temple as your soul.

Who are the buyers and sellers, the money-changers and
dove-sellers, in your soul?

Perhaps today we might speak of these figures as 'the ego':

The parts of us that yearn for approval
that long for affirmation
that want to be in control
that want to dominate and get their own way
that want to be successful.

These things can so easily come to dominate our inner beings;
they can take over from compassion and love; they can become
our identity and deny our vulnerability.

Become aware of Jesus wanting to enter your soul, and finding
that he cannot speak there because it is so full of 'ego'.

Take some stones or marbles and hold each one as you
become aware of ways in which your ego dominates your inner
being:

My desire to be seen as able.
My longings for my children or grandchildren.
My physical strength.
My need to be in control.

These things give us a sense of who we are, and we are afraid of giving them up.

Dare to let Jesus in, to show him your vulnerabilities, to show what you are afraid of letting others see, for only into that fragile space can Jesus enter.

What does the Lord Jesus say?

Today we think about the second half of the passage we looked at in the previous section:

> Well then, in he comes and starts speaking. What does the lord Jesus say? He says what he *is*. What is he then? He is a Word of the Father. In this same Word the Father speaks Himself, all the divine nature and all that God is. (p. 59)

Meister Eckhart sometimes talks of the birth of God in the soul as the 'Word' being 'spoken'. There is a sense in which, in this passage, Eckhart unpacks the first verses of John's Gospel: 'The word became flesh, he lived among us' (John 1:14). This is not theology for Eckhart so much as a living presence that he knows and loves. He *knows* Jesus as the eternal Word, and he *knows* that God is perpetually speaking God-self into our very beings. And he wants us to know it and experience it.

Read John 1:1–3 and 14:

In the beginning…
Was the Word…
The Word became flesh…

Then reread the above passage from Eckhart. Let your imagination open itself to the enormity of what Eckhart is trying to convey: 'In he comes [to your soul] and starts speaking.'

If you have time today, go for a walk.

Look at the trees, at their roots.

Look at the fields, the pattern of landscape.

Feel the age of the land around you.

Imagine generations of people who have lived and worked there.

Become aware of life going back through the ages.

God's eternal Word, spoken, as John tells us, from 'the beginning', has lived and moved through generations; and wants to be born within *us*.

Ask for God's grace, and for humility, that this Word may indeed be born within.

Silence

We have thought about the eternal birth of God within, and yesterday looked at it as God speaking his Word in our souls. None of this is possible, however, unless we are silent and emptied: 'The very best and noblest achievement in this life is to be silent and let God work and speak within. When the powers have been completely withdrawn from all their works and images, *then* the Word is spoken' (p. 7).

'You must cast aside all your deeds and silence all your faculties, if you really wish to experience this birth in you' (p. 22).

How do we become silent? We are so full of chatter, either internal or external. Even when we are not speaking, the voices in our heads go on; our thoughts are busy. Yet, 'you must… silence all your faculties if you really wish to experience this birth…'

Sit down today, to be silent. To pray. To 'be'.

As soon as you sit down, you realise how hard it is to be silent.

If silence is new to you, don't try to sit for too long. Five or ten minutes is enough to begin with.

Sit with your feet flat on the floor, your back reasonably straight. Become aware of your breath, and concentrate on that. You may find it helpful to use a word, to keep your mind focused. Some find the Jesus Prayer helpful: 'Lord Jesus Christ, Son of God, have mercy on me.' Others have their own words. Return to your own word or phrase as soon as you become aware of your mind getting busy again. Let it become like an anchor, holding your busy mind as silent as possible. It isn't easy, but don't despair: keep returning to your word. Remember again, 'The noblest achievement in this life is to be silent and let God work and speak within.' Trust the silence, even though you fail. Trust it, again and again and again.

Emptying

From the silence that we thought about in the previous section, we carry on today to think about being emptied.

> A man cannot attain to this birth except by withdrawing his senses from all things. (p. 25)

> This above all else is needful: you must lay claim to nothing! Let go of yourself and let God act with you and in you as He will. (p. 33)

> The more barren you are of self and unwitting of all
> things, the nearer you are to Him... The true word of
> eternity is spoken only in solitude, where a man is a
> desert and alien to himself and multiplicity. (p. 42)

This self-emptying, or letting go, is not easy for anyone; yet it is perhaps the ultimate message of the mystics.

What does it mean, for those of us engaged in ordinary life?

We cannot let go of our responsibilities, our work, our care of children or the elderly, our care of each other or the earth.

It is to do, rather, with an inner attitude, a lessening of interior clutter. Often we have so many things going round and round in our heads that we are unable to see clearly.

As you sit to pray today, first become aware of the things that keep popping into your head: worries, annoyances, plans, responsibilities.

As you become aware of each of these, simply take them and look at them; put them to one side and tell them to stay there for a while. It may be helpful to 'hold' them in your hands, like a bundle, and then 'put' them to one side.

For the duration of your prayer, you can leave these things to one side; leave them in God's hands, so as to allow space for God to enter.

They will soon find their way back: that is one thing you don't need to worry about!

You may be surprised to find that you feel rather bereft without them: don't worry about this feeling, but be aware that this 'letting go' is not necessarily easy.

Reflect on Eckhart's phrases above. In this way, as Eckhart says, you will find 'much true guidance in regard to things of which before [you] knew or understood nothing' (p. 17).

Union

> God in all His works has a most blessed end in view,
> namely Himself: to bring the soul and all her powers into
> that end—Himself... For this the Father bears His Son in
> the soul. (p. 18)

> All things become simply God to you, for in all things
> you notice only God. (p. 45)

Union, or oneness, with God might be Meister Eckhart's rallying cry. It is something that he experiences and longs to convey to his listeners. His sermons abound in different words of scripture, as he plays around with language and concepts, in his efforts to share what he delights in, this absolute knowledge and experience of God and self in divine union.

> 'God lies in wait for us,' he says, 'with nothing so much
> as with love. For love resembles the fisherman's hook...
> just watch for this hook, so as to be blessedly caught:
> for the more you are caught, the more you are free.' (pp.
> 46–47)

Bring to mind times in your life when you have experienced a sense of being taken beyond yourself: perhaps in art or great music, magnificent countryside or at times of intense emotion.

Recognise such moments as moments of God, not to be clung to, but to receive with grateful heart, and to lead you on to ever greater love. Eckhart says at one point that rather than praying to God to ask for anything, 'I will pray to Him to make me worthy to receive' (p. 101).

You may like to play some piece of favourite music or gaze at a painting or simply watch the clouds crossing the sky, as you meditate on these words from Eckhart:

> In this birth God streams into the soul in such abundance of light, so flooding the essence and ground of the soul that it runs over and floods into the powers and into the outward man. (p. 16)

Receive from God what God is eternally offering you.

Unknowing

> For all the truth learnt by the masters by their own intellect and understanding... they never had the slightest inkling of this knowledge and this ground. This may be called... an unknowing, yet there is in it more than all knowing and understanding without it, for this unknowing lures and attracts you from all understood things, and from yourself as well. (p. 11)

Eckhart is part of the great tradition of 'knowing God in unknowing'. As with so much of Eckhart, if we try to understand this with our rational senses, we are doomed! But let it read as poetry in your depths.

All of life, for Eckhart, is shot through with God. God is in every blade of grass, every breath we take. Yet God is ever beyond anything we can say about God.

So as we finish our journey with Eckhart, let's revisit: the birth of God in the soul, God's eternal self-giving, the soul's eternal receiving: the *mystery* at the heart of our humanity.

Consider, and pray with, these words, the first from Paul, the other from Eckhart:

It is no longer I, but Christ living in me. (Galatians 2:20, NJB)

Why did God become man? ... In order that God may be born in the soul and the soul be born in God. (p. 215)

Wrap your thoughts around them as you explore the mystery.

Elijah: encounters with God

Helen Jaeger

Who?

We are about to start a journey with Elijah through 1 Kings 17—19. You may like to read these chapters before we begin.

Elijah himself goes on a journey of discovery—most importantly, a journey to and with the living God, who is not always predictable, but who is always loving.

As we prepare to begin this journey in the company of Elijah, let's pause for a moment and ask ourselves this question: 'Who is God for me, and who am I for God?'

Reflection

If you had to choose ten words to describe yourself now, what would they be?

If you had to choose ten words to describe God, what would they be? Maybe you could find images to accompany your ideas. If you put the two lists together, what does this look like? Can you see areas where your relationship with God is strong—or areas where it is weaker? What might God be saying to you about any of those areas now?

Standing up for God

In 1 Kings 17, Elijah addresses King Ahab, with whom he will have a running conflict throughout 1 Kings 17—19. Elijah's message is brief and to the point.

> *'As the Lord, the God of Israel, lives, whom I serve, there will be neither dew nor rain in the next few years except at my word.'*
>
> 1 KINGS 17:1, NIV 1984

Note how Elijah's statement is rooted in his relationship with God: 'the God of Israel, whom I serve…'

Reflection

If you were to stand up for something for God, what would it be? Whom might you confront? What might you say? Consider how you could complete the statement, 'By the Lord, whom I serve…' Ask God to guide you and inspire you.

Finding God in creation

In 1 Kings 17, Elijah discovers that God uses creation to look after him with water from a brook and food from ravens. Too far-fetched? What if you found that God could use creation to bless you, provide for you, nurture you or inspire you?

Reflection

Take a faith walk. Schedule in some time to walk in a place of beauty near you. It doesn't have to be a special place, just a place that contains something of God's creation. Take a camera, notebook or sketch book with you. As you walk, allow your eyes to fall on whatever you naturally notice. What thoughts and feelings rise to the surface as you do so? Let yourself pause with what you are drawn to—a tree, perhaps, or birdsong, or the shape of a leaf or tree bark or mud. Perhaps thoughts, feelings or prayers arise in you from this natural contemplation. Don't force it, but allow the response to happen naturally. Can you believe that this experience might be God gently whispering to you through the beauty of creation? What is he saying? Record God's voice with your camera, sketch book or notebook.

Encountering the poor

Elijah is camping out near the brook of Kerith, where he's been miraculously fed by the ravens. Suddenly the brook he was drinking from dries up. What does Elijah do? Believe that he heard God wrong? Complain against the Lord for sending him to some God-forsaken wilderness? No, he listens some more.

This time, God gives Elijah a new directive: go to Zarephath in Sidon and stay there. 'I have commanded a widow in that place to supply you with food' (1 Kings 17:9). Elijah, obedient to the voice of the Lord, heads off for Sidon. As he reaches the city gates, he sees a widow gathering sticks. Does the widow recognise Elijah as some man of God she's seen in a vision, since the Lord has already told Elijah that she will give him food? Hardly!

Elijah calls out to her, 'Would you bring me a little water in a jar so I may have a drink?' (v. 10). The widow obediently sets off to fetch it, and as she does so, Elijah calls out again, 'And bring me, please, a piece of bread' (v. 11). This is too much for the widow. '"As surely as the Lord your God lives," she replied, "I don't have any bread—only a handful of flour in a jug and a little oil in a jug. I am gathering a few sticks to take home and make a meal for myself and my son, that we may eat it—and die"' (v. 12).

What does the prophet hear in her voice? Desperation, perhaps? 'Don't be afraid,' replies the man of God, reassuring her. 'Go home and do as you have said. But first make a small cake of bread for me from what you have and bring it to me, and then make something for yourself and your son. For this is what the Lord, the God of Israel, says: "The jar of oil will not run dry until the day the Lord gives rain in the land"' (vv. 13–14).

God proves Elijah right, and God, Elijah and the poor widow come into something like a holy triangle of provision: God provides for the widow, the widow provides for Elijah and Elijah strengthens the widow, ultimately in raising her only son from the dead (vv. 17–24).

Reflection

Imagine a person you know who is 'poor'. This could be materially poor, spiritually poor, morally poor or physically challenged in some way; certainly someone who you feel is vulnerable or needy. Bring that person before your eyes in your imagination. See them in the fullness of who they are. Now imagine that they have a gift to give to you. Let them open their hands to show you this gift. What do you see? What are they holding? Let them speak. Open your ears and hear what they have to say. In humility, receive what they give you, as though it is in fact a gift from the Lord.

You may already have had this experience of receiving from people who are 'poorer'. Many involved in charity work comment that it is they who are the recipients of life, care, encouragement and joy from the people they work with. You may like to consider how you can develop this disciplined, humble openness to God and other people around you.

Acts of mercy

Have you seen the film *Schindler's List*? Based on real events, it tells the story of Oskar Schindler, a German businessman, who saved the lives of more than a thousand Jewish refugees, mostly Polish, during Hitler's years in power.

In 1939 the Germans moved Polish Jews to the Krakow Ghetto in Poland. Oskar Schindler arrived in the Polish city, hoping to make a profit from the war. As a member of the Nazi party, he bribed his way into favour with SS officials and acquired a factory to produce military kit. He hired a collaborator, Itzhak Stern, a member of the Jewish Council, to help him. Schindler decided to hire Jewish Poles to work in his factory, as they cost less than other workers.

Stern began to ensure that as many Jews as possible were saved from transportation to concentration camps. Not long after the factory opened, new SS officials arrived in Krakow to build a new concentration camp. In the process, they arbitrarily murdered anyone they wanted to, including old, ill and vulnerable Jews.

Schindler, a witness to these events, was profoundly affected by what he saw, but had to appear on side with the SS. Despite this, he covertly began to save as many Jewish lives as he could. He and Stern compiled a list of workers, for whom inclusion on 'Schindler's list' literally meant the difference between life and death.

For the remaining war years, Schindler was engaged in a twin process of protecting as many innocent lives as he could, while simultaneously bribing Nazi officials and buying munitions from other factories to cover up the lack of production at his own. He ran out of money as the war ended. However, his grateful Jewish workers sent him off with his own letter of protection and a ring engraved with a Talmudic quotation, 'Whoever saves one life, saves the world entire.'

In 1 Kings 18, we meet the figure of Obadiah, who is a little like Schindler. Obadiah is employed by Ahab, the dictator of Elijah's time, as master of his palace. When Jezebel, Ahab's corrupt wife, was 'killing off the Lord's prophets', Obadiah had secretly 'taken a hundred prophets and hidden them in two caves, fifty in each, and supplied them with food and water' (v. 4).

Obadiah was not the main player in the story of Elijah, but what he did affected the lives of a hundred people. (It's estimated that there were at least 6000 descendants of people saved by Oskar Schindler by the time he died.)

Reflection

As you read the biblical account in 1 Kings 18:2–19 and think about the modern film, what strikes you about the similarities between the two stories? Next, can you think of instances in your own life when someone with apparently divided loyalties acted on the side of right and justice—perhaps a boss at your workplace or a politician or maybe an atheist friend or someone who said they were against you, but turned out to be for you after all? Today, meditate on the question: 'What small thing can I do for the kingdom of God today?' It doesn't have to be big, but, like the actions of Obadiah and Schindler, it may prove to be significant.

The power of persistence

It's no accident that Elijah is called a man of faith. Read 1 Kings 18:41–46, noting how Elijah persisted as he waited for rain to end the drought.

Three years ago I fell sick with a mystery virus. For several weeks, doctors scratched their heads over what was wrong with me, as I got progressively worse. First they tried this kind of medicine, then that. Finally they gave up. 'You'll just have to get better in your own time,' they said. 'But I feel really sick!' I feebly complained. They ordered more tests, prescribed more drugs. Nothing seemed to make any difference. Unused to a lethargic and ill me, a few friends dropped away, and some family members urged me to get up and get going. I couldn't. The mystery illness had me in its grip. All the energy and motivation that had been a part of me drained away completely.

I read the Psalms: 'You lay me in the dust of death' (Psalm 22:15). How true this felt! This dry, dark, barren place of illness was my whole experience. My faith was seeping away, too.

Finally, one of my doctors gave me good advice. 'Start slow,' she advised. 'Just try to do a little more each day. That's how elite athletes rehabilitate themselves—little by little. We don't know entirely what caused this, but this is the path for you.' I started to follow her advice. I was weak, but by some grace of God, determined.

A particularly compassionate friend came and walked round the block with me. Another came and regularly had lunch with me. A third prayed for me, since I was finding praying particularly hard. I started to go swimming, just a little, twice a week.

That was three years ago. Three weeks ago I completed a 100-length swim for charity, and a friend of mine handed me a brochure for triathlon events, suggesting I have a go. I've written three books and travelled recently to Spain with family. My faith has somehow returned. What made it possible? The grace of God and grace-filled persistence. Was it easy? No. Did I have to be persistent? Yes. Was it worth it? Absolutely.

That doesn't mean to say that we won't have periods of weakness—we will. That we won't have periods of illness, perhaps severe illness—we will. That we won't have difficulty, disappointment and failure—we will. But focusing on an end goal, persevering—seven times if necessary, like Elijah's servant—will help to pull us through, even to heaven itself through death, if necessary.

Reflection

Vision boards are an effective way to set goals and develop discipline. To make a vision board, collect images and quotes that inspire you for the area or areas of your life you want to address (for example, faith, family, health). (If you want to use an online tool, http://pinterest.com/ works well for this.) Put the images and ideas together and write out a simple goal, for example, 'I will run three times a week.' Include a statement about why you want to do this. It's particularly powerful if you can bring your spirituality into it, for example, 'To this end I labour, struggling with all his energy, which so powerfully works in me' (Colossians 1:29). Place your vision board somewhere prominent where you will see it often. Allow it to inspire you to persevere towards your goal.

Getting to the heart of fear

In 1 Kings 19 we begin to read about the vulnerable side of Elijah. Here is a courageous prophet who has listened attentively to the word of God and found God looking after him and all his needs. Not only this, but when he confronted a bunch of corrupt religious 'prophets' in front of the whole of Israel, the

God he publicly prayed to sent fire to consume Elijah's water-drenched sacrifice. This was not for showmanship, but because Elijah passionately wanted Israel to return to the true God. Could Elijah receive any greater seal of approval?

Immediately afterwards, Elijah prophesied to Ahab that the drought that had held the land in a vice-like grip for three years was about to break. And he was right! You would think that Elijah would be on an unstoppable 'faith high' after these events. Yet, when word comes from Ahab's vicious wife that she intends to seek and kill him, 1 Kings 19:3 tells us that 'Elijah was afraid and ran for his life'.

Reflection

As you look back at your life and faith journey so far, can you spot high points—times when God was obviously present? Maybe there are other areas of your faith or life where you are uncertain or afraid. Take a sheet of blank paper. Write on it, 'I'm afraid…'. Now put next to it the first thing that comes into your head. Continue this, until you've exhausted every thought of fear that you have. Can you take your fears to God in prayer, sharing your vulnerability? It may feel uncomfortable at first, so ensure you are in a safe and quiet place as you do so.

Is God in the drama?

Having taken himself far into the desert, Elijah hides in a cave. Now, perhaps, he's over his suicidal thoughts and possibly his despair (1 Kings 19:3–5), but he's still as far away from the action as he possibly can be. Word comes to him from the God he loves in the form of a simple question: 'What are you doing here, Elijah?' (v. 9).

Elijah answers God honestly. In essence, he says something like, 'I've stood up for you, despite all the corruption around me; there's no one left, and now they're trying to kill me!' (see v. 10). What does God reply? 'It's OK, I love you', 'Don't worry, you did a great job', 'OK, fine, stay in the cave'? No, God says to the weary and bruised Elijah, 'Go out and stand on the mountain' (v. 11). God is about to pass by.

1 Kings 19 tells us that as God passed by there was a hurricane, an earthquake and a fire—but God was not in any of these things.

Reflection

Perhaps you have been or are currently in a situation in your life that feels dramatic, but maybe you are struggling to find God in it. Can you name that situation—a bereavement, breakdown, tragedy, redundancy, illness, conflict at work? As you honestly look at that situation, is there a part of you that wonders if God is behind it? Is there a part of you that blames God for it? (It's very natural for us to feel this way.) How might it change your feelings about the situation to believe that God is not 'in' that situation as such, but may in fact (as we see with Elijah later) have a different way to be with you—and also a plan to help you?

Or is God in the gentle whisper?

In 1 Kings 19:12–13, we find that it is only at the sound of a 'gentle whisper' that Elijah comes to the entrance of the cave, covering his face with his cloak. This gentle whisper, this new tender embrace, now asks Elijah the same question, 'What are you doing here, Elijah?' (v. 13).

Reflection

Sit in a quiet, enclosed place. Quiet your mind and heart. Now imagine a gentle whisper coming to you personally, addressing you, your life and your faith with no judgment and only love: '(Your name), what are you doing here?' Perhaps you can make a creative response, or perhaps you just want to sit quietly and answer privately to the God who loves you in the depths of your vulnerable heart. Allow whatever emotions you feel to rise to the surface, whether they are positive or negative. Do not rush this. There is no one to judge your answer, and what you say is not about performance, but about truth—the truth that will ultimately set you free.

Prayer of quiet

Why does God choose to address Elijah from a gentle whisper? It's a good question to ask. Your answer and mine may differ, which is OK, too.

My personal view is that with all the drama that's been happening in Elijah's life, a pep talk from an omnipotent deity is the last thing Elijah wants right now. He needs comfort and reassurance. He doesn't need big, 'shouty' events—he needs love and tenderness. You can almost hear the plaintive tones of his complaint: 'I am the only one left!' (1 Kings 19:10 and also 14)—and perhaps, underneath it, the unspoken question, 'God, do you really care?'

When you fall in love, it's said, you don't just do it once, you do it many times over, as you discover more depths to your beloved that you did not know existed previously. God is in a process of wooing Elijah, and Elijah is like you and me—he's on a journey of discovery about the God of love that will last his whole lifetime and beyond.

Reflection

Elijah was at a particularly vulnerable point in his life and faith. What does your life and faith look like at the moment? Bring that before God in prayer. Can you imagine that God wants to touch that place? It may be painful or joyful. Be ready to receive. Stay in that place, possibly without words, in an attitude of prayer, for as long as you can. Be open before God and allow your vulnerability to be touched by his tenderness.

God has a plan

Experts say that in good parenting, active listening is a crucial skill. Even when a good parent sees that their child is in pain—and knows the solution to it—it's important for them to encourage the child's expression of it.

God certainly does this with Elijah, asking, 'What are you doing here?' Now comes the solution.

The Lord said to him, 'Go back the way you came, and go to the Desert of Damascus. When you get there, anoint Hazael king over Aram. Also, anoint Jehu son of Nimshi king over Israel, and anoint Elisha son of Shaphat from Abel Meholah to succeed you as prophet. Jehu will put to death any who escape the sword of Hazael, and Elisha will put to death any who escape the sword of Jehu. Yet I reserve seven thousand in Israel—all whose knees have not bowed down to Baal and whose mouths have not kissed him' (1 Kings 19:15–18).

God has listened. What if God is waiting for you, too, to unfold everything that has been happening to you—yes, even the worst bits—and afterwards wants to show you a plan of action?

In another place in the Bible, King David (who is hiding from his persecutors in a cave, just like Elijah) says: 'I pour out my complaint before him; before him I tell my trouble' (Psalm 142:2).

Reflection

Here's a suggestion for how to apply this to your own life. Take a sheet of paper. Write or draw on it all the things you are worrying about. Fold it up. Now place yourself in a position of prayer. Deliberately unfold your paper and allow God to see it, perhaps holding it open in front of you in a symbolic gesture. Can you discern anything God might be saying to you about what you've expressed? Maybe thoughts or Bible verses come to mind. You could jot these down on the reverse side of your paper. Allow more thoughts to arise in the days and weeks that follow.

Mapping the journey

As a way of finishing our journey with Elijah, we're going to map where he has been and where he has encountered God, before we apply the same process to our own journey of the last two weeks.

In Elijah's story there are significant moments and places where he encounters the living God: Kerith, Zarephath, Mount Carmel, Beersheba (gateway to the desert), Mount Horeb and the desert of Damascus.

Are there significant places you can think of where you have encountered God on this adventure of faith?

Reflection

Draw or compile a map of your encounters with the living God as you have journeyed with Elijah, and perhaps include a brief description of what happened or what you learned. You could also include tentative notes about the places to which you think God might be directing you next, just as Elijah heard the call to continue in 1 Kings 19:15–18.

Let your map ultimately be a celebration of this ongoing journey of life and faith, encounters with the living God, that every person of faith has—Elijah and you, too. And believe that there is more to come.

Travelling with St Francis

Sally Welch

An introduction to St Francis

It is dawn in Assisi, a small medieval town in the middle of the hilly central Italian province of Umbria. The air is cool and fresh at the moment, but the clear blue sky promises another hot day. No one is to be seen in the narrow streets, edged with houses whose brightly coloured shutters catch the eye in the midst of the dark stonework, black with the dirt of ages. The houses are crowded together, jostling for space, top floors overhanging the streets. Here and there a space is clear round the tower of a church standing cool and aloof from the humble dwellings around it. Later in the day the streets will throng with the noise of guided tours and the shouts of shopkeepers selling souvenirs and postcards. The dim cool passageways will flash bright with digital cameras, and queues for the churches will snake along the roads. But now, in the stillness, it is possible to catch a glimpse of the spirit of St Francis, wearing his coarse brown woollen robe, with a pair of shabby sandals on his feet. He is singing to himself a canticle of praise to his God, and his heart is light because he is setting off along the path that leads through Gubbio to Laverna, and a retreat house where he will stay for the period of the Lent of St Michael (from the Feast of the Assumption, 15 August, to the Feast of St Michael, 29 September).

There he will spend time with God, for whom he has abandoned so much and from whom he has received even more.

What can the life of an indigent monk, a failed soldier, a man disinherited by his parents, who spent his life in relentless travelling, driven by who knows what inner compulsions, say to us, living in today's world? Why should we listen to a man who danced on the very edges of life? It may seem almost ridiculous to be drawing on the life of such a person to help us find a spiritual path through the complex network of moralities, values and goals that are set before us today. Yet there is something about this man, the intensity of the life he led, the purity of his relationship with God and his creation, that draws us to him, encouraging us to seek within his words and his actions a primer for our lives today.

A spirit of poverty

Matthew 19:21; Luke 9:3, 23

From the very beginning, poverty has been a cornerstone of Franciscan spirituality. St Francis himself stuck rigorously to his complete abnegation of all possessions. He, and later his band of followers, either worked or begged for the small amount of food they needed to sustain life, and they gave away the rest, or all of it if it was required by someone in more severe circumstances than they were in. No doubt influenced by his childhood in the house of a merchant to whom material possessions were not only a symbol of status, but in themselves the means by which more was accumulated, Francis saw all material goods as obstacles to a life of communion with Christ. Liberated from the struggles to acquire and the fear of subsequent loss, Francis would move lightly through the world, unhindered by baggage.

For most of us today a similar dramatic shedding of all our material goods and responsibilities is inadvisable. But there is a middle way that treads carefully through a landscape cluttered with unnecessary material and status objects, taking them without linking oneself to their value, appreciating them without becoming defined by them, sitting lightly to the benefits and disadvantages that they bring. Living a life of Franciscan poverty means surrendering ourselves to the will of God. We need not be afraid of enjoying God's gifts, but we must always bear them lightly and be ready to share them or give them away. This can be a frightening thing to do, and it is not always immediately apparent how to begin this way of life. Try making a note of everything you spend on yourself in the coming week—cups of coffee, outings, treats. At the end of the week, give the same amount to your favourite charity and spend nothing beyond what is absolutely necessary the next week. How difficult is this for you to do? What do you feel? Has this changed the way you will spend your money in the future?

God's love for his creation

Before you begin, go outside and gather five bits of vegetation in various stages of growth and deterioration.

St Francis wrote the 'Canticle of the Creatures' at the end of his life when he was in constant pain. Despite this, the poem is filled with joy. This first section celebrates Francis' close relationship with the natural world, and his recognition of its mutual dependence with the people who live in it.

The Italian weather is unceasingly varied. These changes are integral to the survival of the landscape. So, too, are the times and seasons of our lives, each changing, each important in its own way. Take the five pieces of vegetation that you have gathered, and carefully place these in front of you. Look at them closely, and notice how unique each of them is. Remind yourself that all God's love went into creating those plants. God loves them; they are irreplaceable. Marvel at the miracle that created them. Remind yourself that God loves you, that all his love for creation was poured out in creating you, redeeming you for his own.

Consider where in your life you are: are you a young shoot, or are you showing signs of ageing? Think of the joys associated with each season of your life. Reflect on your spiritual life: are you in the same place as your physical life, or are you as yet unfruitful, still a seed? Or perhaps you feel your spiritual life to be dead and needing to be revived. Ask God to help you blossom spiritually in whatever season of life you have reached. Thank him for the joys of your life and also for the sorrows—in themselves as important to growth and flourishing as times of gladness. Gather your bouquet together and leave it where you will be able to see it throughout the day, giving thanks whenever you do.

> *Most high, all powerful, all good Lord!*
> *All praise is yours, all glory, all honour, and all blessing.*
> *To you alone, Most High, do they belong.*
> CANTICLE OF THE CREATURES, PART I

Francis kisses the leper

Imagine you are journeying with St Francis through the hot, dusty countryside of Umbria. The day is warm, the road long. Your companion is quiet and thoughtful; he is trying to work out exactly what God wants him to do with his life. Your eye is caught by a shapeless form clothed in rags, slumped in the middle of the road. This wretched, dirty object can only be a leper, the sufferer of an incurable, disfiguring disease that condemns the victim to a life of exclusion and isolation followed by a miserable death. You want to avoid him—leprosy is contagious—but you are even more worried about Francis; he has a pathological fear of people with leprosy.

Francis looks up and sees the woeful figure. Across his face flit a number of emotions. First there is terror, then something that seems to be resolution. Francis urges his horse onwards, and you follow, but from a distance; you have no idea what will happen next. Francis dismounts his horse, then, his face rigid with determination, reaches out his hand to the leper. In return, the poor ragged man stretches out his deformed hands; he is hoping for some alms, but instead his hand is taken gently and he is brought to a standing position and then embraced by the young, well-dressed man in front of him. In wonder, the leper receives a kiss and more money than he thought possible. But the beggar is not as amazed as you are, for on Francis' face is a look of such joy and love as to transform it totally. Here is the beginning of Francis' new life, one that has no room for fear or doubt, only great love and trust in God.

What are your feelings as you watch the meeting between Francis and the man with leprosy? Is there some equivalent in your life—a type of person you find it difficult to engage with, a situation that you lack sympathy for? How is God calling you to behave in these situations? How might you react in the spirit of St Francis? Is there some small step you can take today that would enable you to encounter your fears or dislikes and overcome them?

Freely give

Matthew 10:7–10

One day, while attending mass, Francis heard these words from Matthew's Gospel read out. They struck an immediate chord with him: his life was to be one of freedom in poverty and joy, in surrendering all that he had and was to Christ. He adopted the form of the Tau cross as a way of demonstrating his commitment to this way of life. The Tau is the last letter of the old Hebrew alphabet (similar in shape to our letter T) and has been used by Christians from very early times. It was said by the Church Fathers to be the mark that was imprinted on the forehead of the prophet Ezekiel as a sign of God's saving love for human beings: 'Then the Lord… said to him, "Go throughout the city of Jerusalem and put a mark on the foreheads of those who grieve and lament over all the detestable things that are done in it"' (Ezekiel 9:3–4, NIV). St Anthony of Egypt is said to have worn the sign of the cross on his cloak, and Francis' biographers write that Francis was so struck by the sermon of Pope Innocent II on the subject of the Tau that he began to draw it on walls and other surfaces and used it as his only signature to his writings. It very soon became the sign of the Franciscan Order and today is internationally recognised as such.

Read these verses from Matthew 10 and reflect on what they might be saying to you.

Forgiveness

All praise for those who forgive
For love of you and endure humility and tribulation
Happy are those who endure them in peace
For you, Most High, they will be crowned.
CANTICLE OF THE CREATURES

'Father, forgive them, for they do not know what they are doing' (Luke 23:34). Francis' life was harsh and uncompromising, but he counted as joy every tribulation he suffered for the sake of

God. It is unlikely that we will be asked to endure the persecution that is suffered by Christians in other countries, but there will be times when we will be called to endure comments or criticisms, unfair treatment or unpleasant jibes. At such times we can use this verse to ask God for strength and patience.

'Forgive us our debts as we have also forgiven our debtors' (Matthew 6:12). As we expect to be forgiven freely, so we must do the same in our turn. Go for a short walk outside, and as you journey, search for about six pieces of litter. You might want to wear a pair of gloves for this. Alternatively, find some pieces of rubbish from around the house. Put the rubbish in a bag, then look for an old container; a used can or drinks carton is ideal. Find a quiet space and place the bag of rubbish in front of you, next to the container. Pick up a piece of the rubbish and think of an action someone has committed that has hurt you. As you bring it to mind, imagine yourself walking up to that person, telling them what they did and then forgiving them for it. As you forgive them, push the piece of litter right down into the container. When you have brought to mind and forgiven all those who have hurt you, put the container into the bin, saying the canticle verse above, and walk away, without looking back.

The stigmata

It is 1224. Francis is a sick man, with only a short time to live. News of his preaching and work has spread far and wide. Nearly blind and longing for solitude, he has escaped to Laverna, a mountain retreat. Francis arrives on the back of a donkey, accompanied only by Brother Leo, and immerses himself in the healing solitude of the rocky hideaway. Brother Leo is given strict instructions to call on him only once a day by singing the opening words of the service of Matins. If Francis responds, then Leo may join him with food and water. If there is silence, Francis is to be left alone.

Imagine the scene. You are walking in the fresh morning air up a mountain path with Brother Leo. You are carrying some coarse bread and a flagon of water, all the refreshment that Francis allows himself. You can see Francis in the distance, standing outside the cave-like dwelling he has chosen as his retreat. Suddenly you see seraphs with wings of fire, carrying the image of the crucified Christ. They swoop upon Francis as he stands, helpless, and imprint upon his hands and feet the marks of nails. His side bleeds with an open wound. So great is Francis' empathy with the sufferings of Christ that he has been given the privilege of bearing them himself—the first recorded instance of the stigmata. From now until his death, Francis will carry these signs of his holiness.

Many people have a mixed response to the stigmata—the signs of Christ's wounds that appear on people's hands and feet. What do you feel about them?

The stigmata can be a sign of extreme closeness to Christ. Is there some further time of prayer or reflection that might bring you closer to Christ?

Wounds need not be external. Have you ever suffered for your faith? Has this strengthened you or damaged you? Can healing be found in reflecting on Christ's suffering for us?

The first crib

Three years before Francis' death, he arrived at the little town of Greccio at the season of Christmas. Francis, whose passion was to communicate the gospel in ways that all people could understand, was struck by a desire to share his joy at the birth of the Saviour with as many people as possible. Having gained permission from the Pope himself, he found a suitable space, and had an ox and a donkey brought to it, along with a manger filled with hay. Then he gathered his Franciscan brothers and invited all the townspeople to celebrate the birth of Christ at the manger. According to one of his 13th-century biographers, Bonaventure, 'that venerable night is rendered brilliant and solemn by a multitude of bright lights and by resonant and harmonious hymns of praise. The man of God stands before the manger, filled with piety, bathed in tears and overcome with joy'.

From this first live illustration of the incarnation all our nativity plays, crib figures and other scenes derive. It is important that their sheer number and familiarity should not distract us from a true appreciation of the radical nature of this act of love, undertaken by God for all of us, and first shown to a humble people by a man whose nature was as radical as the Christ he followed.

Preach the gospel

Matthew 5:1–12

The story is told of St Francis going down to a village with one of his monks to preach the gospel. When they arrived at the village, they quickly engaged the local folk in conversation and passed their time helping the villagers with their work, sharing stories, entering into the life of the community. As the end of the day drew near, Francis said to one of his companions that it was time for them to return to the monastery. Francis' companions, with great concern, said, 'Didn't we come here to preach the gospel to these people? When are we going to do that?' Francis turned to his brother monk and said, 'If these people have not heard the gospel today, then reading from the Bible will not make any difference to them!'

When Christians show mercy, act as peacemakers in their community, and seek God, they do not do so because they are merely 'nice people' or because they want to get to heaven. We do these things because we are called to continue the work of Jesus, to act as his hands and his feet on this earth until his kingdom is seen here once again. And we don't content ourselves simply with speaking about God's loving kindness, but we actively take the gospel wherever we can. As St Francis himself is reputed to have said, 'Preach the gospel everywhere; if necessary, use words.'

'Remember that you might be the only Bible people read' goes a well-known saying. If other people encountered Christianity only through your actions, what might they think of it? What would they think Christians believed and how might they think Christians behaved? Reflect on your actions over the past 24 hours, and try to recall any instances where what you said and did were gospel actions. Think of those occasions where your behaviour did not 'preach the gospel'. How could you have behaved differently? Resolve to spend the next 24 hours with an increased awareness of your role as a preacher of the gospel.

Approaching death

All praise be yours, my Lord, for our Sister bodily Death
From whose embrace no mortal can escape.
Woe to those who die in mortal sin.
Happy are those she finds doing your most holy will
The second death can do no harm to them.

CANTICLE OF THE CREATURES

In a society that has few taboos left, death is the last great secret of all. Focusing all their energies on staying young, many people spend little time, if any, considering that most inevitable of events, their death.

Find somewhere comfortable to sit, in as quiet a place as possible. You should have a pen and paper near at hand. Now close your eyes and imagine that you are approaching death. Ask yourself, if you were to die now, which actions would you regret not having done, and which would you wish you had? Which experiences have you left to do that you always thought you had time for, and how important are they now that you have no time left at all? Who do you wish to be at your bedside and what would you say to them? Spend as much time as you need to think of all these things, writing them down if you want to.

At the end of this time, draw a picture of a gravestone on the paper. If this was your headstone, what would be written on it? Be as truthful and realistic as possible. If you need more space, try your hand at writing your obituary as it might appear in your local newspaper or parish magazine.

Once you have written the words, reflect on them.

Now imagine that you have one day left to live. What will you do with all your regrets and unfinished business, your vocations that were unfulfilled? Write these down in order of importance. What would you change about your obituary? What would you like to have written?

Now recall yourself to your normal life. In view of what you have felt, what are your priorities going to be in the future? In the face of your regrets, what are you going to change about your life in the future?

Prayers of St Francis

My God and my all

May the power of your love, Lord Christ,
Fiery and sweet as honey,
So absorb our hearts
As to withdraw them from all that is under heaven.
Grant that we may be ready to die for love of your love
As you died for love of our love.

Lord, make me an instrument of thy peace.
Where there is hatred, let me sow love.
Where there is injury, pardon.
Where there is discord, vision.
Where there is doubt, faith.
Where there is despair, hope.
Where there is darkness, light.
Where there is sadness, joy.
O divine Master,
Grant that I may not so much seek to be consoled as to
console;
To be understood as to understand;
To be loved as to love;
For it is in giving that we receive,
It is in pardoning that we are pardoned,
And it is in dying that we are born to eternal life.

The Franciscans

During his life, Francis established the order of Friars Minor—a
group of men who lived lives of poverty and holiness, following

a strict Rule. Later, with St Clare, he founded the Poor Clares—nuns who lived in similar communities to the Friars Minor. However, even during his lifetime, Francis was asked how he could help those people who were married and living in the secular world and who expressed a need to grow in holiness and commitment to God. Accordingly, he founded the Third Order of Franciscans, also known as Tertiaries. Today, there are over half a million Franciscans—followers of St Francis—worldwide. These include men and women of the First Order, who live celibate lives within their communities, and also members of the Third Order, men and women living out in the world who are called to a Franciscan Rule of Life that encompasses the Franciscan values of prayer, study and work.

Tertiaries show us that a spiritually committed life can be lived out in the world just as well as in a monastic environment. Battles with the temptations of the world can be fought and won without having to retreat to solitude and isolation apart from the world. The battle may be fierce and the victory harder won, but it is none the less a victory that is within our grasp.

As part of becoming a Tertiary Franciscan, every novice has to develop a rule of life. This is a serious undertaking; it is not just a plan for how we would like things to be, but a way of measuring one's way of life. It involves every aspect of life, not just the obviously 'spiritual' parts. It is a means of growth and transformation and can form a strong supporting structure for change.

You might like to think about writing a rule of life for yourself. This should be undertaken seriously and followed for a specific length of time before reflecting on how you have changed and whether the rule should be altered.

Try to think about the different areas of your life and develop a rule for them. Areas to consider might be:

- Prayer and worship
- Health and leisure
- Relationships and community
- Study
- Giving

Ask for God's help in working out your personal rule of life, and start with the least you believe you can do; you can always make changes later.

Glimpsing the kingdom

Janet Lunt

Thresholds of the kingdom

> *Not everything has a name.*
> *Some things lead us into the realm beyond words…*
> *It is like that small mirror in the fairy tales—*
> *you glance in it and what you see is not yourself;*
> *for an instant you glimpse the Inaccessible,*
> *where no horse or magic carpet can take you.*
> *And the soul cries out for it.*
>
> ALEKSANDR SOLZHENITSYN, NOBEL LECTURE 1970

An experience or revelation of God is irreplaceable. It is a gift. It may take a person by surprise and be life-changing. More often, it arrives in small ways, perhaps in prayer and worship, through 'coincidences', through words coming alive.

People who came across Jesus during his life on earth glimpsed the 'Inaccessible'. We might also call it heaven, otherness, the eternal, or the invisible God. Jesus talked about the kingdom that was not of this world, and to describe the indescribable he used metaphor, imagery, parable and poetry. His word-portraits of the kingdom of heaven illustrated a way of living of the highest good, for humanity to engage with as a prelude to an eternal future.

Perhaps you have sensed something powerfully good or a holy 'otherness' in someone you have met that you attribute to the presence of God. In the Gospel encounters with Jesus, we discover that many were drawn to Jesus—to listen, to be with, or willingly to leave everything and follow.

What leads us into that realm beyond words, the realm of understanding or of encounter? Alongside the teaching of Jesus and the rest of scripture, many things can 'speak' to us, and like that fairy-tale mirror become thresholds to glimpses of the kingdom. Examples might include nature, beauty, sermons, books, music, compassion, experiences, fellowship, stories. Difficult experiences have also led many to encounters.

Reflection

What draws you to Jesus? Tell him in prayer.

Call to mind the thresholds through which you have glimpsed the unseen God or understood more of the heavenly kingdom. Let a piece of your favourite music transport you into thankful prayer.

You may like to ponder whether you think all things could be potential windows or doorways to the eternal.

Ears to hear, eyes to see

Jesus taught as if the ordinary existed to explain the extraordinary. Speaking largely in parables, he used everyday images such as vineyards, house-building, bread-making, weddings and plants to communicate eternal things. And he often added, 'Let anyone with ears to hear listen' (Mark 4:9, 23; Luke 8:8; 14:35, NRSV).

If we discern the meaning of his stories for ourselves, it not only brings illumination but is also a faith-building experience; we own it because it is like finding hidden treasure. Jesus' words to Thomas might be appropriated here: 'Blessed are those who have not seen and yet have believed' (John 20:29, NIV). We may also discover further layers of meaning as we ponder a parable. And if one seems like a riddle, it is encouraging to know that the disciples sometimes had to ask for explanations (for example, Luke 8:1–15). One thing is clear; we need ears that hear and eyes that see. The men who followed Jesus in Matthew 9:27–30 were blind and yet they 'saw', for they addressed him as son of David, meaning that they believed he was the Messiah.

The Bible is shot through with instructions to seek insight, wisdom and understanding. God gave a large amount of these qualities to Solomon, 'as measureless as the sand on the seashore' (1 Kings 4:29, NIV), a gift that drew many from other nations to experience it, notably the Queen of Sheba. The King James Bible replaces 'understanding' with the compelling phrase 'largeness of heart'. How vast and measureless, then, must be the heart of God who gifted Solomon.

Reflection

Pour some dry sand (if you have none, try salt, couscous or sugar) on to a tray, and spend some time running it through your fingers. Wonder at the creation of sand from the remains of creatures and rocks, the wearing down by weather and waves, and the length of time taken to produce such tiny fragments. A cupful would be impossible to count. Let the image of God's largeness of heart overwhelm you.

Block your hearing and sight for a few minutes. Release them and enjoy the effect of light and sound afresh. Read Proverbs 2:1–5. Invite God to open your inner ears and eyes to discover more of the extraordinary in the seemingly ordinary; perhaps through something or someone you take for granted in your home, fellowship or workplace.

The small door to the topsy-turvy kingdom

He who gathers virtues without humility is like someone preparing and carrying powdered spices in the wind.

ST GREGORY THE GREAT (540–604)

In my youth, I came across this sentence: 'There are two doors to happiness: a mind that is always open to learn and a heart that is always open to love' (source unknown). I wrote it in a new notebook which became a collection of favourite poems and sayings. Above the sentence I glued a picture of a leaping dancer, which somehow seemed appropriate. Reflecting on it now, I recognise that for the heart to stay open it requires humility and grace. It is the path of hope that leads ultimately to freedom and contentment. Staying open is often painful, too, but crucial for growth. To maintain openness in heart and mind, I need to bend—many times.

To enter the church of the Holy Nativity in Bethlehem, one has to bend, as its entrance is a small, low doorway in a vast and ancient stone wall. A minister friend believes there is deep significance in this, because it takes humility to bend the knee to God, who came to us as a vulnerable baby. I am reminded of the small gate and narrow road that leads to life and that only a few find (Matthew 7:14). Indeed, at the heart of Christianity we find the extraordinary mystery of a great but hidden God who is the designer of an upside-down kingdom. Jesus, the king-servant who rode into Jerusalem on a donkey, and whose only crown was of thorns, said something like this: 'You cannot get into God's kingdom, unless you accept it the way a child does' (Mark 10:15, CEV).

Reflection

Spend some time thinking about the words of Jesus from Mark 10:15, reviewing your attitude to humility, learning and openness.

Try to rekindle the wonder of a child throughout the week. Allow yourself to 'play' for the sheer pleasure of the experience—perhaps paint with your fingers, or blow bubbles, or dance around your home to some joyous music.

A small, hidden door

Alice was about to enter Wonderland (in *Alice in Wonderland* by Lewis Carroll). Her boredom on that afternoon had suddenly turned to burning curiosity as the White Rabbit passed—the talking kind with waistcoat and pocket-watch. Alice followed, diving down a rabbit hole without a second thought. After falling in slow motion, she came upon the famous hall of doors and a tiny golden key. Eventually, she found a very small door, hidden at first, which the key unlocked. A tiny passageway revealed to Alice a glimpse of 'the loveliest garden you ever saw'. But not until the end of chapter seven would she negotiate her size successfully enough to fit through the small door leading to the beautiful garden of bright flowers and cool fountains.

For years, I have been working on a large, self-designed tapestry of Alice's discovering the small door—one of several artistic attempts to portray the scene. Over time, this image has spoken to me about my relationship with God's kingdom: I have glimpsed something of another world, as if through a door that is too small to pass just yet, there is a place I long to reach. I journey in a 'land of wonder', a topsy-turvy world where the least shall be the greatest, where the worst crime can be forgiven, where healing might happen. I find the ups and downs of faith comically described: Alice finds a key that fits the door, but when a potion shrinks her to the right size, the key is out of reach; then, too much of a magical cake makes her too large and she floats to sea in her tears.

The cameo snapshot of Alice's finding the little door beckons me to share, through my artistic gifts, what I have glimpsed of the heavenly parallel world. These gifts, in turn, have been small doors or windows on to glimpses of God. 'Here's a small door. Come and look through—can you see the beautiful garden? It looks so peaceful and colourful, and is always sunny. At times all is still; at other times music can be heard like bubbling water. You might catch sight of the Master, although you could mistake him for a gardener. He is the one with scarred hands. If not, you know he isn't far away, because there will be signs of work in progress. On occasion, people bask in the sun, while others are helped while they are convalescing; and sometimes, there is a garden party with food fit for a king.'

Reflection

Think of a time when you felt great anticipation, perhaps about to enter an unknown place, opening a new book, or watching the curtain lift on a stage set. Allow yourself to recapture the sense of anticipation you felt. Ask God to recreate this feeling as you pray for the kingdom to come and God's will to be done in you… in the church… in the world.

Imagine walking in the garden of the Lord, as if in the unspoilt garden of Eden, perhaps using reflective music (for example, Vaughan William's *Fantasia on a Theme by Thomas Tallis*).

Small beginnings

Find a small seed, if possible a mustard seed, one that will grow into a large shrub or tree. Find a quiet place and still yourself.

Holding the seed in your hand, think about its potential… as fully grown, any culinary uses…

Ponder the invisible, sleeping DNA instructions within.

Now imagine the seed growing from its tiny, hard, lifeless form into a seedling with twin starter leaves and a delicate white root; see it develop into a sapling with stronger twiggy stems, a mesh of roots and many leaves. Over time, the main stem thickens into a firm trunk and branches spread from all sides at all angles. Watch it become a small, prolifically leafy tree, protective enough for birds to hide their nests in its maze of branches. Flowers appear all over it and, in turn, produce fruiting seed-cases.

Let the sense of miracle take its full effect.

Reflection

Read the parable of the mustard seed (Mark 4:30–32), a story of small beginnings. Jesus does not scorn the small or the simple. Prayerfully allow the imagery to speak to you: of smallness; growth; potential; time; of an unforced process; of God's role; of vision.

You may like to consider the following questions: what might be the significance of the man planting the seed? What do you understand of the kingdom of heaven through this illustration? Think about your part in this slowly burgeoning kingdom.

Like a tree

Have paper and pen to hand.

You, like a seed-become-tree, are also a miracle. Bearing in mind the slow but sure growth of a tiny seed, consider your faith life as the growing process of a tree. Recollect, if you can, your spiritual germination. What roots have you put down, and where? What keeps you stable and firm in dry times? With branches in mind, what have you reached out and up to in the past, and what new branches are extending and growing at this time? Remember occasions when you have been fruitful for others or provided shelter, and how you have achieved this (for example, when someone felt safe to confide in you). Remember those times when you have received sustenance and love from

God, like rain or sun… and any times when you have withstood wind and storm, or a long winter.

> *'Blessed is the one who trusts in me alone; the Eternal will be his confidence. He is like a tree planted by water, sending out its roots beside the stream. It does not fear the heat or even drought. Its leaves stay green and its fruit is dependable, no matter what it faces.'*
> JEREMIAH 17:7–8, VOICE

Reflection

You may find it helpful to draw a tree or a mind map, and write your thoughts in and around it. Spend time reviewing your spiritual growth, praying for any areas that need attention.

Conscious that you are a miracle, turn your thoughts and feelings to adoration of God.

Hidden treasure

Find and read Matthew 13:44–6, and if possible 'The Bright Field' by R.S. Thomas (from his *Collected Poems 1945–90*, Phoenix Press 2001, p.302; or *Threshold of Light*, ed. A.M. Allchin and Esther de Waal, Darton, Longman & Todd, 1986, p.9; or online, including Thomas reading the poem on YouTube).

The term 'inciting moment' is used in literature to describe the essential event or turning point that sparks the central revelation of a story. This term might describe the initial encounters with treasure of the merchant and man, as well as our discovery of thresholds to the heavenly kingdom. These encounters are potentially transforming, but we need to act to make the treasure or revelation lasting.

In his poem, R.S. Thomas draws upon these treasure-finding parables. He speaks of sunlight breaking through cloud to light up a field and of the need to turn aside to this brightness, like Moses to the burning bush, for it is the threshold to the treasure. He weaves into the imagery his realisation that life is not about hanging on to the past nor impatiently looking to the future. It is about living with eyes and ears attuned in the 'now', where we can experience 'the eternity that awaits you'.

Find a quiet place to sit. Consider how you remember your past—do you tend to dwell on or in it? And your future—do you view it with expectations, hope, impatience, fear? Note your thoughts and feelings, then let them go. Relax, valuing the present moment, the 'now', as being all that you truly have. Be alive to its sacredness, and open to God. Stay with it as long as you are able, ready for whatever comes, be it simple mindfulness or burning bush.

Creature comforts

Moths, mice, woodworm, burglars, gas leaks, fire and flood—all can threaten our homes and belongings. For some, war and oppression strip them of all they have. Yet we readily forget that everything we own—clutter, necessities and comforts—could be lost in an instant.

Jesus spoke of storing up treasure in heaven, the kind of 'possessions' of which rust, creatures and thieves cannot deprive us (Matthew 6:19–21). Two thousand years on, we live in a very different society, and we are bound to own many things. Money brings choice, and we are great believers in choice. Our society runs on it. The news informs us daily of which way the scales are tipping, and exposes the consummately greedy while applauding highly paid celebrities. Money can feed hungry mouths, but also status, indulgence and greed. Jesus warned against the power of money, which is able to distract us from kingdom living and community. The poet and mystic Angelus Silesius (1624–77) wrote: 'A wealthy man obsessed with profits, deals and losses is a poor wretch; possessing nothing, he is in truth a man possessed.' Money and possessions are merely transient gifts.

Read the parable of the rich fool in Luke 12:14–21.

Although parallels could be drawn between the rich fool and a senior banker legitimising fat bonuses during austere times, we all need to reflect on mammon and our mortality from time to time. Sadly, for many, it is only in the context of great change, loss or impending death that the power of money loses its hold. In following Jesus, it is judicious to take stock of what we have and how much we share. We need to check that we are not holding on too tightly to what is truthfully God's, and ensure that we are storing lasting treasure.

Reflection

Have a conversation with Jesus about ownership, stewardship, security, letting go, generosity, and so on. Bring any dilemmas that you have with money to him in prayer. Pray for world monetary systems, and for organisations such as Fair Trade that work within it for justice.

Meditate on Jesus' words about our treasure being where our heart is (Matthew 6:21).

You could visit the website www.rejesus.co.uk to see a commissioned painting by Jim Janknegt of the rich fool, and listen to Jim's video diary.

Behind closed doors

The Lebanese spiritual writer Khalil Gibran (1883–1931) has provided a helpful reflection on the belongings with which we fill our homes. Spend time considering the following excerpt on 'Houses' (or read the complete section in *The Prophet*, William Heinemann Ltd, 1972, pp. 26–28, also available online).

What is it you guard with fastened doors? Have you peace, the quiet urge that reveals your power? Have you remembrances, the glimmering arches that span the summits of the mind? Have you beauty that leads the heart from things fashioned of wood and stone to the holy mountain?... Or have you only comfort, and the lust for comfort, that stealthy thing that enters the house a guest, and becomes a host, and then a master?... But you, children of space... you shall not be trapped nor tamed. Your house shall be not an anchor but a mast. It shall not be a glistening film that covers a wound, but an eyelid that guards the eye... For that which is boundless in you abides in the mansion of the sky, whose door is the morning mist, and whose windows are the songs and the silences of night.

A good balance

'Therefore every teacher of the law who has become a disciple in the kingdom of heaven is like the owner of a house who brings out of his storeroom new treasures as well as old.'

MATTHEW 13:52, NIV

Many years ago, I participated in a renewal week in my church. We spent time together in a three-fold way: remembering how God had blessed us in the past, learning creatively in the present, and seeking vision for the future. Later, in my local home group, members shared the blessings of the week. One very old man was unable to take part in the week through frailty. He had been heavily involved in church renewal in his past and was sad to miss the events, but with immense humility and grace he listened and commented, then told us finally that his renewal had come through our sharing. The words of Jesus about the teacher of the law (or the 'good scribe') immediately sprang to mind, seeming to encapsulate the week, the evening and the frail man's life—a helpful image of balance between past and present inspiration.

Reflection

When Jewish people put on their prayer shawl, they often recite a prayer ritual, using words of prayers and of familiar verses from the psalms. Two psalm sections of this ritual are as follows: Before the shawl is put on, they inspect it and say the first two verses of Psalm 104. After they have wrapped the shawl round them, they use the words from Psalm 36:8–11. You might like to begin and end your prayers today using these verses.

Alternatively, use a prayer from the past as a frame for your own intercession, praise or supplication. Let it inform and inspire you.

Called

Imagine yourself in a market square, sitting with the disciples in an excited crowd who have been listening to Jesus speak. He sits down to rest and turns to your group. Read through Luke 12:35–38 slowly, as though Jesus were speaking just to you and the other disciples. Listen intently. Note your response and be aware of any questions you might want to ask Jesus.

Think how you might describe the kingdom of heaven to someone who doesn't know about it.

Have a go at rewriting the parable you have just read in a modern-day setting, or create a parable of your own about God's kingdom.

Reflect on this fable. A story is told of a traveller who, while investigating a stone quarry, asked some of the labourers about their work. The first stone mason said that he was cutting stone. The second responded that he was earning five dollars a day. But the third stone mason replied with a radiant face: 'I am building a cathedral.'

An example of a modern parable: the kingdom of heaven is something like this. A squirrel hoards acorns and buries them in many different places for the winter months. During the hard, cold season, some of the acorns are found and eaten by other creatures. Others begin to sprout in the ground, starting their journey of growth into tree-hood where many creatures will rest and nest in years to come. The squirrel forgets where it has hidden a proportion of his store. However, it recovers a good number of acorns, enough to sustain it until the fairer weather.

The eternal dimension

In cinematic photography, it is possible to experience two amazing visual effects: one is time-lapse footage, which shows speeded-up growth or transformation; the other is 'frozen' time, in which synchronised cameras enable the viewer to orbit an object that appears miraculously poised in mid-air (perhaps a water droplet or leaping person), creating a 3D sensation. These techniques enable us to 'see' in a new way.

As we absorb the many images Jesus uses, a fuller picture of the kingdom of heaven begins to emerge and we develop a new way of 'seeing'. We move beyond the familiar dimensions of space and time into a new dimension of values that come from eternity and also lead to it. It is mind-stretching to attune to God's vision and to apply our insight in transformed living. We are in essence invited to live with one foot in eternity.

Something of this mind-stretch is perhaps captured in the words of the classic 'Rainbow Song', created in 1955 by Arthur Hamilton for children. It invites you to 'listen with your eyes' and to 'sing a rainbow'—magical words carried by simple, effective music. A rainbow has an ethereal quality: we see it, but cannot hold it. Similarly with music: we hear it, but cannot see it. If we were to borrow the Rainbow Song's imagery, we could describe Jesus' multi-faceted portrayal of his kingdom as 'singing a rainbow'.

Reflection

Read about the creation of Narnia in *The Magician's Nephew* by C.S. Lewis (HarperCollins, various editions available) (from the sixth page of chapter 8, '"Hush!" said the Cabby…' to approximately the fifth page of chapter 9).

Or spend time with a painting that speaks to you of the heavenly dimension. Respond creatively, with coloured pencils and paper, paints or fabric scraps.

Or recall or listen to a recording of a Christian song or hymn that has inspired you. Note what qualities, vision or values of God's kingdom are expressed. Find a space alone to sing it to God with all your heart, mind and strength.

Journeying with God

Sue McCoulough

Starting the journey

Some of us will journey physically this summer—travelling by plane, train, car, even on foot, perhaps crossing seas by ferry or ocean liner.

Images of sea travel stir up powerful and diverse emotions in people. The prospect of discovering new lands, even navigating rough seas, is exciting to the seasoned boat traveller. Others would find such journeys a nightmare. Many people prefer to reach their destination quickly or at least voyage through calm waters. Of course, some sea destinations can be restful. Holiday brochures often depict paradise as lying on a beach in some remote, sun-kissed island—a prospect other travellers would find uncomfortable or boring.

Even those who don't enjoy travel or the seaside can be enticed by the unpredictability of the sea. One day near a beach, you might watch the waters gently ebb and flow, inviting you to stroll along the sands. Hours later, the same tides might pound against sea walls—exciting viewed from a distance, but terrifying if you became submerged in it.

Over the next two weeks we'll be looking at travel images in the Bible, particularly images connected with the sea, exploring positive and more challenging aspects of 'journeying with God'. André Gide (1869–1951) said, 'One does not discover new lands without consenting to lose sight of the shore.' We all have 'safe shores' that we tend to cling to, and in different ways resist any 'new lands' God would have us travel. Journeying with Jesus won't necessarily take us physically beyond our front door, so the housebound can respond just as well to his call, 'Follow me,' for he calls us on a lifetime's spiritual voyage.

There are times when emotionally it might feel as if we're strolling by a gentle shore with God. At other points we might feel that we're 'drowning' in uncharted territory, submerged by challenges. Where is God for us in these times? Is he only present when we're by calm streams? In Genesis, God is described as the loving creator, making all things out of nothing. From the earth 'formless and empty' came the Spirit 'hovering over the waters' (Genesis 1:2, NIV). We're told that the sea, like all creation, 'was good' (v. 10).

Initially, Old Testament imagery about the power of seas might seem negative. The story of Noah and the ark (Genesis 6—9), the parting of the Red Sea (14:15–22), Jonah and the whale (Jonah 1—2): all these journey narratives start with people being hurled into a deep, destructive abyss with little chance of survival. Importantly, each voyage changes when the traveller starts to move with God's strength and speed.

Whatever form your journey with God takes, he wants you as his travelling companion. Let's place him at the helm and enjoy this mini voyage together.

Imagining voyaging with God

Let's begin with an early biblical account of God on the high seas—Noah and the ark. Read Genesis 7 and 8, allowing the events to unfold in your mind's eye. See yourself entering the ark as part of Noah's family (we are all technically his descendants). Hear God telling you that you're special, worthy to board the ship. Consider taking some aspect of creation with you: other family members, animals, birds or keepsakes that have special significance for you, or will help you to 'stay afloat'. Then consider one of the ideas below:

St Thérèse of Lisieux (1873–97) said, 'Jesus, your love is an ocean with no shore to bound it.' As the flood waters rise, the land disappears. All you can see is water. Immerse yourself in the mystery of God, thanking him for his limitless love.

Traditionally arks can be refuges, safe spaces to encounter God. Imagine your 'creation' ship, lifted high above the earth by waters that cover the highest mountains. You might feel invigorated, scared or perplexed. Recall God's promise to deliver you, even if you're temporarily soaked by upheavals in your life. Notice anything that anchors you as you ride the waves.

Later, the sun emerges from behind clouds, revealing a rainbow. Through this, Noah was promised a fresh start. God might be offering the same to you, revealing himself to you in colourful new ways. Recommit to journey with him in trust and hope. If it helps, draw or paint whatever the rainbow represents to you.

Alternatively, you might visualise your ark experience ending unpleasantly. If you are feeling damaged or dismayed, your vessel might be battered by the waters. Seeing natural disasters on the news, such as flooding in Britain and abroad in recent years, makes us wonder how any good can come out of such catastrophes. Being submerged by difficult situations or illness can seem equally devastating at the time. If this is your physical or spiritual experience, recall that God travels with you, encouraging you to ride the waves with him. Allow any fears and negative thoughts about people or situations to surface in this bumpy journey. Share them honestly with God.

Perhaps for you, this sea has opened the floodgates of emotion, brought tears or laughter. Welcome God in whatever form he approaches you. As with Noah, he longs to establish a new and everlasting covenant with you. Hand over anything that is still unresolved in your mind, or seems damaged beyond repair. Pray for confidence that in God's time and ways, transformation will begin.

You could mark this fresh covenant with God by drinking a glass of water or taking a shower and recalling the cleansing, refining power of God.

St Brendan

The British and Irish are island people, used to charting dangerous seas and unknown territory. Reputedly one of our greatest early explorers was a sixth-century Celtic saint called Brendan. Legends say that he made an epic voyage from Ireland's west coast, reaching America a thousand years before Columbus.

Before attempting the journey, we're told, Brendan prayed and fasted. Enthused by the Celtic symbol of the Holy Spirit, the wild goose, he visualised in his mind's eye the bird, urging him to spread his wings and discover other lands. The quest was physical *and* spiritual—physical because Brendan wanted to glimpse other parts of God's 'paradise', spiritual because of his strong desire to spread the gospel. With 14 other monks, Brendan set sail across the Atlantic, in a flimsy coracle probably made of wood and ox hides, sealed with animal fat.

The story goes that these men encountered fine weather in the first two weeks of the voyage, so only had to steady the sail. But as the wind fell, they were forced to row, day after day. *The Life of Brendan the Voyager* (written in the ninth century) claims that when their strength failed, Brendan comforted the monks with the words, 'Have no fear, brothers, for God is our captain and our pilot, so take in the oars and set the sail, letting him blow us where he wills.' The crew landed at last on an island where streams of water gushed down from the hills. Food was abundant there, so they celebrated Easter, lifting their voices up in songs of praise to God, apparently accompanied by seabirds chirping in perfect harmony. After resting for 40 days, and with God's wonderful provision of a further 40 days of supplies, the monks celebrated Pentecost, embarking again on the wide seas.

St Brendan's prayer

Read this prayer attributed to St Brendan, thinking how you might make it your own.

> Help me to journey beyond the familiar
> and into the unknown.
> Give me the faith to leave old ways
> and break fresh ground with you.
>
> Christ of the mysteries, I trust you
> to be stronger than each storm within me.
> I will trust in the darkness and know
> that my times, even now, are in your hand.
> Tune my spirit to the music of heaven,
> and somehow, make my obedience count for you.

Sailing into the unknown

Following St Brendan's example, our journey takes us into uncharted waters with Jesus. Go to any place where there is water, or sit somewhere quiet where you can imagine the sea. The Gospels of Mark (4:35–41), Matthew (8:23–27) and Luke (8:22–25) have parallel accounts of Jesus stilling the storm.

Shut your eyes and breathe in. Then hear, or imagine you hear, the tide rolling in. Breathe out and imagine the waves receding again. Repeat several times.

Now see yourself, either alone or with others, in a boat with Jesus. Consider firstly how you feel being with him—calmed, excited, confused or apprehensive? Respond as Jesus invites you to take the helm.

The Sea of Galilee isn't renowned for its calmness; however, at this point the water is quite still. Jesus lies down on a cushion and falls asleep. At first you might breathe in deeply, enjoying the cool night air, anticipating a peaceful journey.

But suddenly everything changes. A storm approaches, seemingly out of nowhere. The wind blows up fiercely, whipping up mountainous waves. Within seconds, you are swamped by water sweeping over the bow. Visualise it flooding your vessel, even driving it towards the rocks. Then relate that storm to any turbulent situation or relationship faced by you or by someone known to you.

Turn to face Jesus, lying at the rear of the boat, still sleeping like a baby, apparently not caring. Is he powerless to act in your storm? Could there be a reason why Jesus has chosen to sleep through it? Perhaps trusting you or others to cope with more challenges as his growing disciples?

Whether your faith in Jesus' rescuing power remains strong or not, imagine yourself handing the situation fully over to him. Cry out, 'We're going to drown.' At last his eyes open and he leaps to his feet, demanding bizarrely that the wind and waves 'be still'.

If calmness comes immediately, receive stillness into the

situation you were focusing on during the storm. If calmness seems slow in coming, ask Jesus to show you ways to help you steady your boat.

Close by writing down any insights from this meditation, asking for wisdom to hold on to any promises.

Circling and flowing prayer

Find some water to walk around or, if that's not possible, imagine circling a pool of water. As you do so, reflect on your prayer life. Consider whether you have a regular, flowing relationship with God or feel stuck in a routine.

Water can speak of our emotional relationship with God: famously the woman of Samaria was cleansed by 'living water' when she met Jesus at the well (John 4). Take one of the ideas below.

Imagine dialoguing with Jesus about your current life. Ask for 'living water' to wash away any specific sins that seem to cling to you right now. Visualise being washed by Jesus, and note your response.

Ask Jesus how you can stop 'circling' around waters that don't lead to new life. Where could you be led to fresh streams?

Most of us benefit from asking to receive more 'living water'. This might take the form of balancing different elements of your life better, such as work, rest and prayer time. Or 'living water' could be given to you as the gift of patience or self-control in response to some person or situation. If you sense your need in any area of your life, ask Jesus to give you his living water.

Now break your circling path and wander freely. Perhaps explore an unfamiliar route. Focus on details around you; allow God to speak to you through them. Your senses might pick up new images, sights or sounds. Ponder how God might be speaking to you through these, thanking him for any insights as you conclude walking.

Water in scripture

Light a candle and place a bowl of water in front of it. Look at the light, then its reflection in the water. Ponder some of the following texts as you do so.

> *Christ loved the church and gave himself up for her to make her holy, cleansing her by the washing with water through the word.*
> EPHESIANS 5:25–26, NIV

Allow these words to wash over and refresh you or someone you know who is going through a 'dry' time.

> *With joy you will draw water from the wells of salvation.*
> ISAIAH 12:3

Jesus is saving and purifying you; now wash your hands or splash your face with water from the bowl.

> *'Come, all you who are thirsty, come to the waters; and you that have no money, come, buy and eat! Come, buy wine and milk without money and without cost.'*
> ISAIAH 55:1

Think of people in the world thirsting for God's practical relief to come to them. Imagine the free water of Jesus washing over them. Then think of the spiritually thirsty, needing to receive the 'living water' of Christ, and imagine the water of Christ washing over them.

> 'Whoever drinks the water I give them will never thirst. Indeed, the water I give them will become in them a spring of water welling up to eternal life.'
>
> JOHN 4:14

Absorb Jesus' promise. What situations in the next few days might need that spring of water to recharge you? Close by drinking some water.

Ask to be immersed in Jesus' love as you extinguish the candle.

Water and the psalms

Many psalms use the metaphor of water, either to indicate God's cleansing influence, or to show how he might deliver his people from negative influences. We read of 'floods of life' that might stand for our external enemies, worldly problems or simply personal sins that divide us from God. Even if we seem up to our necks in such things, ultimately the psalmists assure us they're no match for our powerful God.

In this exercise, try focusing primarily on the positive aspects of water: how its power reveals God's strength and renewal even when the world threatens to engulf us. Pray with the opening three verses from Psalm 1, Psalm 23 or Psalm 42. Sense how God might want you to flourish or be protected with these images.

Now write or draw how the calmer waters depicted in the

psalm could speak peace into any tricky situation or relationship you face. Reflect on what 'enemies' can teach you—for example, those who have challenged or hurt you unexpectedly. Close your prayer time by thanking God for his everlasting and nurturing power.

Adventuring with God

Celts like St Brendan had a strong image for the Holy Spirit's action; his 'wild goose' vision inspired St Brendan to travel confidently. Many scripture images tell of the energy and power of God, and praying with these can help to transform us both as individuals and members of the Church. But experience reveals that God's energy and transforming power rarely takes us quickly to places we'd like to go, still less in comfortable, predictable ways.

I once voyaged with a group of fellow pilgrims to an island off the coast of Wales. At first, it was touch and go whether we'd actually get there. A storm was coming, so we had a memorably 'choppy' and wet crossing. At least one of us was terribly seasick!

Storm or no storm, we pilgrims were impatient to get to our destination. Many of you know the familiar cry of a child in the back of the car before you have hardly set out on the road, 'Are we there yet?' Most adults still want to 'arrive', wherever we're going in life. Travelling can be seen as wasted time. As our group agreed with hindsight, the sea's wildness was part of our pilgrimage experience, as memorable as 'getting there'. Journeys such as St Brendan's remind us that life is a series of journeys with no 'arrivals' until we cross that other shore to heaven. God encourages our journeying, whether it's a smooth or rough ride.

When God calls us to travel, we engage in his mission. We

move out of our comfort zone, if only by deciding to cross the road to speak to our neighbour. Many know that strong sense of God's directing them to do something out of the blue. Initially, taking action may seem insignificant. Later, we realise that heeding the call was life-changing, either to us or to someone else—and if the latter, we may never know its full impact.

Once safely arrived on our island in Wales, our group shared stories about dwindling churches and the family or friends who expressed no interest in faith. Sometimes redemption seems to take for ever. But we're never promised a smooth crossing to reach 'the other side'. God won't frog-march us into the kingdom. Whether we're an experienced Christian or just setting out on our faith journey, we can feel excited that God still has new vistas for us to see in 'unknown' territories.

Missionaries pray that their next journey leads them to speak up rightly for God. There's no off-pat script in heaven for converting others, 'bringing back the lost'. Unlike that electronic voice in our car satnav, 'You have reached your destination', none of us reaches our destination while on earth. Knowing that helps us to blend charity with optimism as we think about our own faith journey and encourage others to travel with us.

So I hope to smile more as I anticipate a 'restless journey' to reach God's safe destination, and remember repeatedly that it will all be worth it.

Reflection

How open are you to travelling with God's Spirit, even through choppy waters? Close by spending time letting go and trusting the future to him.

How easily do you let the 'wild goose' lead you to new people or situations? Where might the Spirit be leading you next?

Journeying and prayer

In the Celtic spirituality of these islands, the Holy Spirit stirred up early Christians called *peregrini*. These men and women wandered the countryside and journeyed the seas for God. They left settled homelands at Yahweh's command, following the Old Testament example of patriarchs like Abraham. Like him, they chose to leave behind settled plans, trusting God to govern their journey. They travelled seas without a rudder, so currents, tides and winds took them to destinations known only to their heavenly Father. Even travellers by land often walked to foreign parts with only the Spirit to guide them.

In this exercise, you could do either of the following:

Go to an open space and walk randomly. Remind yourself that ultimately as Christians we are all 'wanderers' on this earth, with no fixed abode (and perhaps thus identifying with those who are literally homeless). How might strolling aimlessly speak of a greater need for flexibility in your daily walk with God? Look around you and spot any fertile new islands, even in places of apparent exile or deadness. Do they prompt you to recognise any areas of your life that might be more promising than you first thought? Write down, draw or pray your insights.

Take a pen for a walk around a piece of paper. Then step back for a while and reflect on the path, perhaps filling in any gaps. Be ready to draw off the page if that seems right. What is God saying to you in this process? Use paints, crayons or felt pens to colour in the gaps between the lines. Consider using colours that suggest the fluid, watery power of God's travelling intuitively through your world. As you colour, allow God to speak to you.

Journeying creatively

Spend time thinking about your life at sea, including where your current location could be. You might see your life as a kind of island, with different areas of fertility or colour. Or maybe you sense that you are on a boat, with Jesus inviting you to launch out in the waters of experience.

If you see life as an island, you could draw a map of this island. As you do, listen to God's call and share with him the gifts of the island.

If you relate to the boat image, you could make a boat (a plastic milk bottle might be a good starting point) or find something to act as a boat. Try sailing your boat on some water. Where is God in your boat?

Artists down the ages have captured the majesty of the sea. Look at some pictures, perhaps re-sketching or writing about something that resonates with you. How might God be speaking to you about your present sea adventure with him?

Listen to some favourite music that evokes images of the sea for you. As you do so, recall the past day's events and detect God's presence in them by using the examen developed by St Ignatius of Loyola.

First, become aware of God's presence. Then let your mind rewind your day back to its beginning, or work forwards from the time you woke up. Recall each step of your day's journey. Try to review the day with gratitude, even if you felt out at sea. Pay attention to your emotions, without judging yourself. Thank God for any anchoring insights. Finally, thank God for that day's journey. Ask for his accompaniment on tomorrow's travels.

Journey liturgy

We journey with you, Father
  As scripture people, ever on the move.
We journey with you, Father
  Through rough seas of sin or misadventure.
We journey with you, Father
  To your 'Promised Land' of true freedom.

Jesus, anchor us in love
  When we feel exiled, longing to reach our
  'destination'.
Jesus, anchor us in love
  When we fear sharing your Good News.
Jesus, anchor us in love
  As we navigate towards the cross, then resurrection.

Accompanied by your Holy Spirit,
  Thank you for the guidance of the 'wild goose'.
Accompanied by your Holy Spirit,
  Assist us through turbulent tides.
Accompanied by your Holy Spirit,
  May we become joyful, fearless pilgrims, even in
  strange lands.

As you pray this liturgy, does any image anchor you in God?
Does any image stir up the 'wild goose' in you towards action?

As a Child

Phil Steer

Welcomes

And whoever welcomes a little child like this in my name welcomes me.

MATTHEW 18:5, NIV 1984, EMPHASIS MINE

For many of us the idea of welcome plays a key role in our understanding of how we relate to God. Seekers are exhorted to 'welcome Jesus into their lives', new believers speak of 'welcoming Jesus into their heart', those seeking to grow in the gifts are encouraged to 'welcome the Holy Spirit'. We think of 'opening the door' to Jesus (see Revelation 3:20), of God coming to make his home with us (see John 14:23), and of the need to let him into each and every area in our lives. And although at times we may wish that we could keep our life as our own, at heart we know that true life is to be found only when we are his.

And so we long for a closer relationship with God, long to welcome God the Father, God the Son, God the Holy Spirit—God in all his fullness. Yet in all our seeking and striving after God, how many of us learn from these words of Jesus, words that teach us how we might go about welcoming him into our lives? For whenever we welcome a little child as he would welcome a little child, then we welcome Jesus himself.

This is perhaps one of those passages that we have a tendency to skip over in our thinking. We find the words encouraging in a vague sort of way, yet do not stop to consider whether they might be anything more than metaphor. Is Jesus simply illustrating something of what it means to welcome him? Or is there some real sense in which, as we welcome a little child, so we also welcome the living Jesus into our lives? And, if that's the case, how might this be?

To begin with, in welcoming a little child we are simply doing as Jesus would do. He demonstrated his great love for little children, welcoming their presence and giving them a position of honour as the 'greatest in the kingdom of heaven' (Matthew 18:4). Whenever we do the same, accepting his teaching and acting upon it, we ally ourselves with him and align our lives with his. In welcoming a child, we welcome the ways of God into our lives.

There is also the sense that, in welcoming a little child, we are welcoming one in whom God's divine nature is more fully present—or, at least, more clearly evident. The book of Genesis teaches that every person is made in the image of God. This is the root of our being, the essence of our nature, and it remains so in every person, no matter how far from God they might stray. Hence, in every human encounter, we are in a very real sense encountering something of the reality of God. Whenever we welcome someone to share our home, our time, our life, we also welcome God. This is true of everyone, young or old; but it is especially true of a little child, where the divine nature has not yet become buried beneath the cares and concerns and trials and temptations of this world.

We can also find that in welcoming a little child we are welcoming one who comes as an emissary of Jesus. Just as a ruler or government will send someone to represent them and act on their behalf, so God sends little children to speak and act for him. In their simplicity and naivety they say and do things that we adults never would, but which can reveal deep truths about the way the world should be, if we only would have ears to hear and eyes to see—'out of the mouths of babes...' (Psalm 8:2, KJV) as the saying goes. God sends children to speak into our world, and by welcoming them, we welcome his word to us.

Since we welcome Jesus when we welcome a little child, so the way in which we welcome little children can teach us and train us in what it means to welcome Jesus. As we become more welcoming to little children, so this fosters within us the actions and attitudes of heart that enable us to be more welcoming to him.

To begin with, we recognise that little children could not care less about who we are in the eyes of the world. Title and status, accolades and achievements, position and power mean absolutely nothing. They do not relate to such external labels but rather to the person that we show ourselves to be in the ways in which we respond to them. And it goes without saying that the same is true of God. As he said to the prophet Samuel, 'Man looks at the outward appearance, but the Lord looks at the heart' (1 Samuel 16:7, NIV 1984). Therefore, as we seek to welcome the person and work of God in our lives, we must set aside such worldly trappings: we must come instead just as we are, prepared to be seen just as we are, and willing to be met just as we are.

When we meet and speak with a little child, we will often bend down or crouch down or get down on our knees—and with a baby we will even lie down flat on the floor. We do this in order to place ourselves at their level, to meet them where they are. We tend to think of kneeling or prostrating ourselves before God as being an act of submission and respect to the one who is immeasurably greater than we are—and this is right, of course. But perhaps there is also a sense in which we are bringing ourselves down to God's level; to the level of the one who has chosen to make himself small, who revealed himself as a helpless baby, and who even as a fully grown man constrained the fullness of his divinity within the limits of humanity. Just as the magi bowed down to worship the infant Jesus (see Matthew 2:11), so must we. When God makes himself small, we have little choice but to make ourselves smaller still.

Having recognised and responded to a little child, we then need to give them our time and our attention—not grudgingly or half-heartedly, with our mind elsewhere and our body eager to follow, but rather giving them the fullness of each moment and the totality of our attention. We need to watch closely and listen carefully in order to recognise and understand the child's needs and desires. We need to join with them in what they are doing, rather than expecting them to join with us in what we are doing. And we need to be prepared for some mess and some noise, for some loss of control, and be willing to accept it rather than trying to prevent it—for a child's thoughts are not our thoughts, and neither are their ways our ways (compare Isaiah 55:8). The parallels with what it means to welcome God into our lives are, I hope, clear to see.

All of this should be an encouragement for us as adults to seek to become more and more welcoming to little children, and through this to become more and more welcoming to Jesus. But of course, by far the best people to welcome little children are not adults at all—however child-friendly we might try to be—but rather other little children. They don't need to set aside the trappings of the world, because they have none; they don't need to make themselves small, because they already are; they don't need to try to relate to a child's way of being, because this comes completely naturally to them. In the same way, it is as a little child that we are best able to welcome Jesus. And so, just as we need to learn to welcome little children as Jesus would do, so we need also to learn to welcome our own 'inner child'. For the more childlike we become, the more welcoming we can be to the childlike Christ.

Spotlight: Introducing the Quiet Garden Movement

Mollie Robinson

As coordinator of the Quiet Garden Movement, it seems appropriate to be writing an article for *Quiet Spaces* because there is a resonance between the Quiet Garden Movement and the creative approaches to prayer fostered in this resource. The natural surroundings of Quiet Gardens provide a context for creativity, for stillness and prayer as well as for the deeper exploration of Christian spirituality.

A garden provides a microcosm of God's presence in nature. Mysteriously, in a natural setting, our souls seem to open more readily and our minds awaken to the voice of God. Christ himself regularly retreated to wild and rugged places to replenish his own resources and to commune with God—and that was in the days before the constant bombardment of noise, social media and access to the internet we have today. Our senses soon become dulled from information overload, and our daily preoccupations are wearying. We easily become vulnerable to endless distractions, and less attentive to our surroundings, to others and to God. Our prayer life becomes the poorer.

It is widely recognised that both adults and children benefit mentally, spiritually and physically from being outdoors. The growth of the number of Quiet Gardens, from the first one in 1992 to the current international spread of well over 300, bears testimony to the fact that many people are recognising the imperative from Christ himself to 'come… to a quiet place and get some rest' (Mark 6:31, NIV). A Quiet Garden is a place where it is possible to leave our preoccupations on one side just for a while. We can breathe deeply, awaken to the birdsong, relish the shy bulb peeping through the earth and wonder at God's creation. Nature has numerous lessons to teach us if we take the time to stop and stare.

Quiet Gardens take many different forms. Each garden expresses this ministry in its own unique way, while simultaneously sharing the core ethos and vision of the Movement to provide local low-cost retreat in a garden venue. The gardens do not have to be pristine nor large, nor in a rural setting—our urban concrete jungles urgently need quiet green spaces!

The key is for the garden space to be available for individuals or groups to come intentionally for a few hours of 'down time'. Each host decides how and what they wish to offer in terms of time and availability. Many Quiet Garden hosts plan Quiet Days, with a facilitator available to give short reflective inputs followed by periods of silence, when participants are free to read, pray, walk or sit in the garden or in an available room. Some offer days of specific creative activity such as painting or writing poetry.

One of the riches of the Quiet Garden ministry is that it can provide a different context in which people can explore their faith. One participant of a garden day, who had long left church life, wrote, 'I had dismissed the serenity, love and courage that God offers to those who listen. The Quiet Garden, and above all the intense gratitude, serenity, love and acceptance that was offered unconditionally, opened my mind to the possibility of a renewed acquaintance with God… The Quiet Garden started me on a second chance at life, offered me a neutral spiritual place.'

Sometimes a Quiet Garden is created specifically to meet local needs. A minister of a United Reformed church in Hackney, London, moved into a manse with an overgrown, neglected garden. She recognised that the local community needed garden space in this noisy, urban, flat-dwelling area. With a few key enthusiastic helpers, the garden was restored, and four areas were created specifically for contemplation. The signs outside the garden now are noticed by passers-by, who respond to the invitation to come in for a moment's quiet pause. Written suggestions for reflection are provided, using the stimulation of the natural world visible in the garden.

And Quiet Gardens are not just for adults. Children benefit hugely from both quiet meditation and being outdoors. Stillness and time spent in a garden helps them to connect with all their senses, to learn about and value the natural world, and to become calm. A school in Derbyshire has developed a garden specifically with those purposes in mind for the local community. A lovely woodland path in the school grounds meanders to a small open area, where benches have the Lord's Prayer carved upon them. The children can write their own personal prayers on a wall as well as enjoying murals of biblical stories. Environmental interest is fostered by the provision of bird boxes, an insect hotel and a small pond.

To find out more about the Quiet Garden Movement, please do email info@quietgarden.org, or take a look at the website www.quietgarden.org, where you'll find a list of Quiet Gardens near you.

Quiet Spaces Subscription

Please note one-year subscription prices below include postage and packing.

You can also purchase your subcription by Direct Debit. Complete the details on the direct debit form and post to BRF with the order form.

Please send *Quiet Spaces* beginning with the September 2014/January 2015/May 2015 issue (delete as applicable).

PRICES FOR UK ADDRESSES

DESCRIPTION	PRICE	QUANTITY ORDERED	TOTAL
Individual 1-year subscription includes postage and packing	£15.99		
Group 1-year subscription postage and packing FREE	£12.75		
ORDER TOTAL			

PRICES FOR OVERSEAS ADDRESSES

DESCRIPTION	PRICE	QUANTITY ORDERED	TOTAL
Individual 1-year subscription Airmail includes postage and packing	£25.50		
Individual 1-year subscription Surface includes postage and packing	£23.25		
ORDER TOTAL			

Prices are correct at time of going to press and subject to change.
For information about group subscriptions, see overleaf or contact BRF at the address given on the next page.

Method of payment

☐ Cheque   ☐ MasterCard   ☐ Maestro   ☐ Visa   ☐ Postal Order

Card no. ☐☐☐☐ ☐☐☐☐ ☐☐☐☐ ☐☐☐☐ ☐☐☐ ☐☐

Shaded boxes for Maestro use only

Valid from ☐☐☐   Expires ☐☐☐   Issue No. ☐☐☐☐
(Switch only)

Security code* ☐☐☐ (Last 3 digits on the reverse of the card)
Essential in order to process your order

0000 **000**
EXAMPLE

Signature .... Date ...... / ...... / ......

All subscription orders must be accompanied by the appropriate payment.
Please note: do not send payments for group orders. All group orders will be invoiced.

Name ....

Acc. No. ....

Address ....

....

.... Postcode ....

Telephone ....

Email ....

If you and a minimum of four friends subscribe to *Quiet Spaces* or BRF's other Bible
reading notes (*New Daylight, Day by Day with God, Guidelines, The Upper Room*), you
can form a group. What's so good about being in a group? You pay the price of the notes
only—postage is free for delivery to a UK address. (All notes are sent to one address.) All
group orders are invoiced. No advance payment is required. For more information, see
www.biblereadingnotes.org.uk/group-subscriptions/ or contact the BRF office.

BRF, 15 The Chambers, Vineyard, Abingdon OX14 3FE;
Tel: 01865 319700   Fax: 01865 319701
www.brf.org.uk   email: enquiries@brf.org.uk
BRF is a Registered Charity (no: 233280)

BRF Quiet Days

BRF Quiet Days are an ideal way of redressing the balance in our busy lives. Held in peaceful locations around the country, each one is led by an experienced speaker and gives the opportunity to reflect, be silent and pray, and through it all to draw closer to God.

Thursday 1 May: 'Watch My Lips…' led by Bridget and Adrian Plass at Scargill House, nr Skipton, North Yorkshire, BD23 5HU

Thursday 22 May: 'What kind of love is this? Living and serving as God's beloved children' led by Tony Horsfall at The Mirfield Centre, Mirfield, West Yorkshire, WF14 0BN

Wednesday 2 July: 'Living in the Secret Place, from Psalm 91' led by Jennifer Rees Larcombe at House of Retreat, The Street, Pleshey, Chelmsford, Essex, CM3 1HA

Thursday 10 July: '"Abba–Father"—the spirituality at the heart of the Lord's Prayer' led by Joanna Collicutt at Harnhill Centre of Christian Healing, Harnhill Manor, Cirencester, Gloucestershire, GL7 5PX

Thursday 21 August: 'Arise, my love and come with me' led by Ann Persson at Carmelite Priory, Boars Hill, Oxford, Oxfordshire, OX1 5HB

Friday 3 October: 'Matthew: his Master's Voice' led by David Winter at Douai Abbey, Upper Woolhampton, Reading, Berkshire, RG7 5TQ

Thursday 27 November: 'Ray of Light: a quiet day for Advent' led by Ian Adams at Mill House, Rochnell Manor Farm, Westleigh, Tiverton, Devon, EX16 7ES

Monday 1 December: 'Mary' led by Andrew Jones at Gladstone's Library, Church Lane, Hawarden, Flintshire, CH5 3DF

For further details and to book, please go to www.brfonline.org.uk/events-and-quiet-days or contact us at BRF, 15 The Chambers, Vineyard, Abingdon, Oxfordshire, OX14 3FE; tel: 01865 319700

Direct Debit

You can pay for your annual subscription to BRF notes using Direct Debit. You need to give your bank details only once, and the payment is made automatically every year until you cancel it. If you would like to pay by Direct Debit, please use the form opposite, entering your BRF account number under 'Reference'.

You are fully covered by the Direct Debit Guarantee:

The Direct Debit Guarantee

- This Guarantee is offered by all banks and building societies that accept instructions to pay Direct Debits.
- If there are any changes to the amount, date or frequency of your Direct Debit, The Bible Reading Fellowship will notify you 10 working days in advance of your account being debited or as otherwise agreed. If you request The Bible Reading Fellowship to collect a payment, confirmation of the amount and date will be given to you at the time of the request.
- If an error is made in the payment of your Direct Debit, by The Bible Reading Fellowship or your bank or building society, you are entitled to a full and immediate refund of the amount paid from your bank or building society.
  - If you receive a refund you are not entitled to, you must pay it back when The Bible Reading Fellowship asks you to.
- You can cancel a Direct Debit at any time by simply contacting your bank or building society. Written confirmation may be required. Please also notify us.

The Bible Reading Fellowship

Instruction to your bank or
building society to pay by Direct Debit

**DIRECT
Debit**

Please fill in the whole form using a ballpoint pen and send to The Bible
Reading Fellowship, 15 The Chambers, Vineyard, Abingdon OX14 3FE.

Service User Number: | 5 | 5 | 8 | 2 | 2 | 9 |

Name and full postal address of your bank or building society

To: The Manager ....

.... Bank/Building Society

Address ....

....

.... Postcode ....

Name(s) of account holder(s)

Branch sort code

☐☐–☐☐–☐☐

Bank/Building Society account no.

☐☐☐☐☐☐☐☐

Reference

☐☐☐☐☐☐☐

Instruction to your Bank/Building Society

Please pay The Bible Reading Fellowship Direct Debits from the account
detailed in this instruction, subject to the safeguards assured by the Direct
Debit Guarantee. I understand that this instruction may remain with The
Bible Reading Fellowship and, if so, details will be passed electronically to
my bank/building society.

Signature(s)

Date

Banks and Building Societies may not accept Direct Debit instructions for
some types of account.

The Blue Reading Fellowship

Instruction to your Bank or
building society to pay by Direct Debit

Please fill in the whole form using a ball point pen and send it to the Blue
Reading Fellowship at: The Grange, Vale, Yeovil, Somerset BA21 4JH

Originator's Identification Number

4	1	5	0	1	2

Name and full postal address of your Bank or Building society

To: The Manager _____ Bank or Building society

Address _____

_____

Name(s) of account holder(s)

_____

Branch sort code

Bank/Building society account number

| | | | | | | | |

Reference

| | | | | | | | | | |

Instruction to your Bank or Building society
Please pay The Blue Reading Fellowship Direct Debits from the account
detailed in this instruction subject to the safeguards assured by the Direct
Debit Guarantee. I understand that this instruction may remain with The
Blue Reading Fellowship and, if so, details will be passed electronically to
my Bank/Building society.

Signature(s)

_____

Date

_____

Banks and building societies may not accept Direct Debit instructions for
some types of account.